Who Ministers to Ministers ?

A study of support systems for clergy and spouses

Barbara G. Gilbert

An Alban Institute Publication

The Publications Program of The Alban Institute is assisted by a grant from Trinity Church, New York City.

Library of Congress Catalog Card Number 87-72687
ISBN #1-56699-022-X

CONTENTS

895 80

ACKNOWLEDGMENTS

My thanks and appreciation go to the many people who helped me with this research and project.

The Institute for Advanced Pastoral Studies of Detroit, Michigan (now called The Ecumenical Theological Center) provided guidance for this dissertation research project which was part of my Doctor of Ministry degree work with them.

My husband, Tuck (Rev. Dr. Chandler Gilbert), was supporter par excellence from the beginning to the end of this two-year project.

Gretchen and Cline Frasier saw me through numerous computer problems in the preparation of this manuscript.

Dr. H. Sook Wilkinson, Rev. Dr. Edwin McLane, Ann Diemer, Rev. Dr. Peter Meek, Rev. Jamie Gustafson, Rev. Jane Henderson, Rev. Dr. Barbara McCall, Deana Kohl read this manuscript and made editorial suggestions.

The Massachusetts Conference of the United Church of Christ supported this research with a financial grant.

Finally, my sincere thanks go to all those persons I interviewed and who shared with me their stories, feelings and knowledge. Their experiences are the heart of this book.

CHAPTER I

In Search of Answers

Clergy, and often their spouses, are in key supportive roles to members of their congregations. They seek to create caring and faith communities where parishioners have ongoing nurture and support for their lives. This support is so crucial that it is one of the clear priorities of pastoral ministry.

Clergy and their spouses experience the same kinds of joy, pain and brokenness as their parishioners. *Where do they turn when faced with personal problems? Who ministers to the ministers and their spouses? Do they find the support they need? If not, why not? If so, where do they find it?*

My interest in these questions has evolved out of my own journey which has taken me through more than thirty years as wife of a parish minister and thirteen years as a professional on the ministry staff of a local church. During these years my husband and I discovered our own need for support as we journeyed through three critical illnesses and a death in our family, through innumerable church crises that contributed to personal and marital stress, and through the many ups and downs that are part of normal living. Along the way we have experienced isolation and support, vulnerability and strength, spiritual highs and lows. There were times when we felt very supported, but there were other times when we felt very much alone and didn't know where to turn for support. All of these experiences heightened my interest in finding out how other clergy and their spouses get the support they need. This became the focus of my doctoral research.

The specific research design, scope and data can be found in Appendix I. But the key questions I am asking are:

1) What are the personal issues facing clergy and their spouses? Have they found or not found support in the midst of them?

2) What facilitates clergy and spouses or hinders them from finding the support they need? What part do individual and so-

cietal attitudes, professional training and judicatory structures play in these helps and hindrances?

3) What are some of the possible directions or solutions for creating better support systems?

The real answers to these questions have to come from the life experiences of the clergy and clergy spouses who are in the local parishes across the country, in the large parishes and small ones, the rural, suburban and urban ones. The answers need to come from the male and female clergy and the male and female spouses, from the married, single, divorced and homosexual clergy. Some of the answers will come from those persons in the seminaries and judicatories who work with clergy.

So I turned to a diverse sample of clergy, spouses and leaders, primarily within the United Church of Christ, and asked them to tell me about their support systems. What is it like these days to be in parish ministry? What is it like to be married to a parish minister? What are the seminaries and denominations doing to provide support? My aim is to tell their stories, because I believe we can learn from each other. In the pages which follow you will find many quotes which highlight their experiences and provide the foundations for some significant learnings.

As I talked with them I discovered that there is no clergy and clergy spouse mold, but a rich variety of individuals and responses to life's experiences. Yet, underlying the diversity, there are some basic issues. I hope that reflections on these issues will challenge us to look a little more deeply at our own experience, attitudes and needs. I hope that they will point us in some new directions for meeting support needs, individually, professionally and within the denominational systems.

CHAPTER II

All Stressed Up and No Place to Blow?

I am appalled at what is required of me. I am supposed to move from sick-bed to administrative meeting, to planning, to supervising, to counseling, to praying, to trouble-shooting, to budgeting, to audio systems, to meditation, to worship preparation, to newsletter, to staff problems, to mission projects, to conflict management, to community leadership, to study, to funerals, to weddings, to preaching. I am supposed to be "in charge" but not *too* in charge, administrative executive, sensitive pastor, skillful counselor, public speaker, spiritual guide, politically savvy, intellectually sophisticated. And I am expected to be superior, or at least first rate, in all of them. I am not supposed to be depressed, discouraged, cynical, angry, hurt. I am supposed to be up-beat, positive, strong, willing, available. Right now I am not filling any of those expectations very well. And I am tired. (A clergyman)

Fidelity to the Christian gospel guarantees extraordinary stress in service. (Lennart Levi, 1967, as quoted in Koval and Mills, 1971, p. 2.)

Pastors take a lot of responsibility for being kind to others, but when they come to taking care of themselves, they are not nearly as kind. (A UCC Area Minister)

Stress and burn-out scores of clergy wives are at least as high as those for the clergy themselves. (Oswald, Jan-Feb. 1984.)

Not having someone to talk with increases the stress. (A clergyperson)

Since studies of stress indicate that the worst possible combination of work conditions is high-performance demand, combined with little control over the situation, the position of the clergy may, by nature, be dangerous to health. (Edwin H. Friedman, 1985, p. 216)

It comes as no surprise to anyone associated with parish ministry that it is a stressful vocation. The reasons for this are legion and vary with the situation and person. Stress is frequently seen as negative, but when stress is of reasonable proportions it can be an invitation to creativity and change. However, when stress is long-term, unresolved or of crisis proportions it may deaden creativity and be destructive of health and the ability to function. Understanding the stresses of ministry can be an open door to using them creatively. The aim is not to avoid all stress, but to understand and use stress as an invitation to personal, professional and systemic change and growth. For the well-being of clergy and their spouses *and* our churches, the stresses of our profession must be dealt with in ways that are faithful and which allow us to persevere over the long haul.

My main focus is to identify ways of finding support in the midst of stresses. However, during my 65 interviews with clergy, spouses and denominational leaders, certain stresses surfaced again and again. Therefore, it feels important at the beginning to take a look at some of the key stresses of parish ministry before addressing the issue of how clergy and spouses can find support in the midst of them.

The stressful issues that clergy and their spouses experience include all those usually experienced by other people in our society: illness; marital and family problems; death and other losses; divorce; depression; anxiety about community and world issues; etc. However, there are some stresses that are directly related to the clergy role per se, and it is on these that I'll focus. It is obvious that not all clergy and spouses experience *all* these stresses, but I believe that the areas of stress which are described below are significant enough and common enough to be acknowledged.

We'll look at the stresses that are specific for: 1) parish ministers; 2) spouses of clergy; and 3) clergy marriages. Finally, we'll look at whether clergy and spouses who are "all stressed up" are able to find places to "blow" in the midst of these stresses. Do they find people to support them in both the normal and crisis times of their lives?

A. Stresses of the Parish Ministry

When clergy are asked what presses them the most, "job-related stress" heads the list. An ecumenical study (Mills and Koval, 1971) indicated that 2/3 of the clergy sampled attributed their stress to work-related issues. They rated the specific stresses in this order: a) personal and ideological conflict with parishioners, and b) over-work, with a frustration of lack of accomplishment (Mills & Koval, 1971). A 1985 UCC survey of clergy, done for the "Clergy in Crisis Study", rates the areas of stress in this way: a) Job related, 54%; b) Personal, 32%; Environmental/Societal, 14% (section II, p. 1). My re-search and interviews with clergy helped me identify some of the specific issues behind these statistics. For example:

1) Expectations and Projections

A great deal of stress focuses around expectations, both external and internal. The expectations that congregations have of their pas-tor are often quite different from those the pastor brings with him/ her when entering ministry. Furthermore, in recent years, with the mobility of the population, the expectations of the people in the churches have increased. People coming from different church backgrounds have varied experiences, and they all bring with them a different set of expectations. The stress level goes up to the de-gree that pastors feel that they must fulfill all these expectations. Ministers often find that the demands of parish life mean that they are spending the greatest amount of time on the tasks they enjoy least and feel least prepared to perform. For example, the minister finds that he/she is expected to be "Chief Executive Officer" of the institution, using up time and energy which the minister would pre-fer to spend being pastor, spiritual guide, teacher, etc.

The expectations of parishioners not only encompass on-the-job time, but spill over into the entire life of the clergyperson. Often at an unconscious level there is an expectation that the minister is the "resident holy man or woman," and together with his/her family will live a model Christian life style. These expectations often are felt more intensely in the small town and in small churches where there is less space between public and private life.

The clergy often serve as a lightning rod for the needs and pro-jections of parishioners. The projections that clergy experience are both positive and negative. One clergywoman spoke of how she was idealized. "They heap extra love on me because of what I *repre-sent to them*, not because of the person I am." Parishioners often want to believe that their minister is a model of their idealized ex-pectations. If clergy begin to believe these idealizations, it results in an inflated self image. If, on the other hand, the clergy fall short of people's idealized expectations or are unconsciously associated with certain authority figures in the lives of parishioners, then they can be the target of many negative projections.

Even more than the expectations of parishioners, clergy often find their own internal expectations to be most difficult. Many clergy hold extraordinarily high standards of performance and achievement, along with a real commitment to be faithful to their understanding of ministry. Yet their vocation allows little opportunity to measure success in the intangible areas of preaching and teaching "the Word" and pastoring. Much of the world and many congregations measure success in institutional terms such as growth in numbers of people, buildings, budgets and programs. How does one feel successful when the expectations and definitions of success are so different and the evaluation process so hard?

2) Role Confusion

Stress exists wherever there is a lack of clarity about one's task or role or value. Role confusion can stem from the differing expectations and goals of the clergy and congregation, as we have just seen. But much of the confusion is also the result of changing times. There is considerably less automatic status granted to the church and to ordained clergy than there used to be. Religion is often no longer the organizing center of people's lives. The values that clergy hold and promote are often quite different from their congregation's. This often results in feelings of powerlessness in the clergy.

Furthermore, the meaning of ordination is less clear than it was. As we seek to foster and honor the "ministry of the laity," and claim ministry for the whole people of God, there is less clarity about what is unique and special about the ordained ministry. Feminist theologians, especially, are questioning the model of hierarchical and authoritative ministry which has often dominated in the past, claiming that this sets up a first class (clergy) and second class (laity) of ministry that is contrary to the one calling we all have by virtue of our baptism (Weidman, Ed., 1984, pp. 79-80).

Finally, there are many models of ministry vying for allegiance: counselor, prophet/social activist, administrator, spiritual director or guide, to mention only a few. We are in a period of redefinition and transition, one that offers new possibilities, yet inevitably is accompanied by confusion and stress.

3) Work Overload

"So much hangs on me" says one clergyperson. "I feel like I have to do everything. I know how that sounds, but that's the feeling." The nature of the job is that it is never done. The needs of the people and of the institution always outstrip the clergy's time and energy. As one minister put it, "There's just too much work. One part of me relishes it, but the other part longs for more space and time for personal reflection, family, friends and interests." Another said, "There is no clear demarcation of where my personal life ends and my job begins. It's a 24-hour job that can't be left at the office." This aspect of being "on call," available for unpredictable emergencies, makes it difficult to order one's work and personal life.

As our society experiences increased levels of stress, there are more demands on the clergyperson's pastoral and counseling time. In addition, this increased stress lowers the availability of the time laity have to share the ministry and often lowers their tolerance for the stress that may take place within the church. All this has ramifications for the workload of clergy.

4) Conflict

According to Robert Kemper, "The primary stress in a pastor's soul is the stress of conflicting groups within the church" (1985, p. 58). The clergyperson, who is often a mediating personality, is drained as he or she tries to be the bridge and mediator between these groups. You will note that 79 of the 149 clergy who responded to my questionnaire indicated that at some time during their ministry they had experienced major conflict with parishioners or staff. (See Appendix IV) One pastor talked about the difficulty of preparing a sermon that has spiritual vitality, or of being fully present to people in need when he was mentally and emotionally preoccupied with conflict.

5) Job Insecurity

Anxiety caused by conflict or by other sources of stress in ministry is often increased because of the nature of ministerial employment. In the ministry, one's economic well-being and vocational position are derived from an occupational system which is almost totally dependent on the approval and good will of the congregation. This can become a strong deterrent to creative risk-taking and experimentation, and often increases tension, especially during periods when there is an oversupply of ministers. The security of having an escape-hatch, such as the confidence that "I can always move to another church if things don't work out," is hard to come by in times like this.

6) Key Career Points

There are certain points in the careers of clergypersons that are particularly prone to extra stress. A first parish is one of these times. Many find that academic training and their own ideals about ministry do not correspond with the reality of the parish. Though field work in a "teaching parish" during the seminary years gives a taste of the reality of parish life, there are few professions where there is such an instant jump from student to *head* of the institution, as when a seminarian moves straight into his/her own parish. Many feel thrust into a situation where their congregations expect them to "know it all" in areas where, in fact, they have had little preparation. For example, I heard several accounts of clergy in their first parish who had no idea how to prepare a funeral or wedding service or provide leadership for stewardship.

Other key stress points are: negotiating a change of parishes, including the terminating and start-up process; mid-life and pre-retirement times; long pastorates; inability to move to another church; and finding ways to exit the parish ministry gracefully.

7) Loneliness and Isolation

At one level, the ministry provides unusual opportunities for being part of a community, and I found many clergy rejoicing in that part of their vocation. Yet there were undertones about how their ministerial role cut them off from people in social situations. Most clergy have experienced awkward changes in a group conversation when they arrived, or have sensed that they are not welcome at certain social gatherings. There is a hunger in most of us to be seen and accepted as persons in our own right, not just in the role we perform. Whenever it is difficult for clergy to find places where they can be out of their role or accepted in spite of their role, they experience isolation.

Loneliness and isolation seemed particularly problematical for specific groups of clergy. For example, a woman minister often experiences extra scrutiny. There is extra stress for many woman clergy in the local parish and among her clergy peers just by virtue of her token status. (This may be true of other minorities as well.) If in addition, the woman is single, the loneliness may be increased. As one woman put it, "At the end of the day, I have no one to go home to. That's when I need someone to talk it all over with and someone to give me a hug."

Another group of clergy that bears some extra isolation are those who are homosexual. Often their job-security may hinge on secrecy about their sexual preference. Lack of social situations where they can be accepted with their partner as a couple, and living under the tension of keeping their sexual preference hidden, takes a toll. For those who are open about their homosexuality, employment opportunities are dramatically decreased.

A third group with special needs are those who are going through personal problems that are common to all of the rest of society, but which are unacceptable to many congregations: marital problems, depression, children on drugs, spiritual dryness, alcohol abuse, family tension, etc. Because of the public nature of the ministry and the subtle belief that clergy and their families should be "better than the rest of us," these issues often bring with them an added degree of isolation for clergy and spouses.

B. Stresses on the Spouses of Clergy

The role of clergy spouse is probably in even more flux than the role of the clergy. The wife of a clergyman can no longer be expected to fit the traditional role. There is also a growing group of male spouses of female clergy who are moving into uncharted waters. The husbands of female clergy and the wives of male clergy have quite different stories to tell. While I will be speaking mainly of the wives of clergy, at the end of this section I will also share what I learned about the role of male spouses of female clergy.

Ministers' wives come in many varieties. Some see themselves as partners in ministry with their husbands; some prefer a supportive, but a less active role, with regard to their husband's ministry; others want nothing to do with the church and ministry at all, leading lives separate from their husbands' careers; and finally, there is a growing group of two-career marriages where the wife is a professional in her own right. Sometimes her profession is also parish ministry, and this may even include being in a team-relationship with her husband. Usually however, her career is totally separate.

Each of these roles has its own particular stresses. Yet, none of these wives can ignore dealing with what it means to be married to a minister. Here are a few of the most common stressors for ministers' wives.

1) Expectations

No matter how clergy wives define themselves, they receive projections and expectations from members of their husbands' congregations. As Roy Oswald puts it: "The clergy wife tends to be seen as the resident 'holy woman': after all she lives with the resident 'holy man.' She's a walking target for everyone's unconscious expectations of what a holy woman ought to be like" (1984, p. 11). Not very many years ago the accepted model of the minister's wife was one in which the wife was an active partner in ministry, or at the very least played a major supportive role to her husband in the church. There was ample advice as to how this was to be carried out: how she should dress, how she should raise the minister's children and what she should and should not do in the church. Many of the clergy wives I talked with expressed the belief that the changing times and the women's movement were easing this old load of expectations. They acknowledged, however, that it is still hard to deal with parishioners' assumptions. For example when the chips are down and the church can't find someone else to do a job at church, "of course" the minister's wife will do it; or "of course" she will be at all of the women's gatherings and be ready to give the devotions at the drop of a hat. One woman put it this way, "If a wife does too much, she is 'running things,' and if she is quiet and reserved, she is not doing her share and fulfilling her role as pastor's wife." Another woman said, "It's interesting that I'm the only woman in the church who is never thanked for doing a job. I like sharing my talents, but it's hard always to have my contributions taken for granted as if I've been hired to do it."

Most wives find that there is an expectation that they can fill in for their husbands as listener and counselor. Many find that having people trust them with their problems is a satisfying part of the role. Others find this a stress factor and an expectation they would prefer to do without.

Quite a few wives claim to feel minimal stress due to these kinds of expectations, but for some they are very real. The wives who are having the least problem are those who had repeatedly defined themselves to members of the congregation, refusing to accept others' expectations of them. Often these women are employed outside of the home, or have a number of small children who protected them from being sucked into the traditional role. The wives who seem to be most affected by expectations are:

1) the wives new to the role of being "minister's wife";

2) those who have chosen to take more of a partnership role in their husband's ministry, but didn't want to be taken for granted;

3) those who are following a minister's wife who modelled a very different role than the one they chose.

2) Finances

Clergy salaries are often very low compared to the salaries of professionals of similar education and responsibility. It is interesting to note that half of all of the clergy spouses polled indicated that they had a major concern about finances. It appears that wives are often more concerned with the finances than their husbands are. One possible reason for this may be that wives are the ones who have to balance the budget and manage the household on minimal funds. Another is that the "clergy script" doesn't allow some clergy to express concern about money. One wife suggested that her husband believed in being the "suffering servant" when it came to salaries.

3) Time for Family and Each Other

One counselor of clergy summed up this stress factor by saying: "Heading the list of perceived needs is the tendency for clergy to put the church ahead of their marriages and families. This is a crucial factor and tends to lead to all kinds of problems including clergy burnout and marital and family disintegration." Lack of time seems to be the major stressor. Fifty-five to 70-hour work-weeks that include work commitments on weekends and evenings were mentioned again and again. Though many appreciated the flexibility of their husbands' schedules and were totally supportive of the ministry, the long hours and the many emergencies meant too little couple and family time. They often spoke about having to be the "primary parent" too much of the time. When our children were small, I recall the depression I felt at the end of vacation time, feeling that I was saying "goodbye" to family time for another year.

Many wives feel that it is not appropriate to complain, because, after all, their husbands are "doing God's work." The more committed a wife is to the church and the ministry, the more difficult it is to claim time for herself and their family. This creates a double bind. She knows there is a need for more family and couple time, but this is in competition with "God's ministry." Consistently coming in second to the demands of the church and the needs of other people is a real stress factor for many wives.

How do they deal with this double bind? Three-fourths of the clergy spouses responding to my questionnaire said that depression had been an issue for them. Forty-two out of 81 claimed to have had feelings of being "trapped" or "stuck." Dean Merrill, in his book *Clergy Couples in Crisis* (1985), offers one possible explanation. The reason depression is so high, he says, is because wives can't find acceptable ways to deal with their anger. Rather than expressing anger, a more common alternative is to deny it and hide in busyness which actually leads to depression.

4) Parsonage Living

Living in a parsonage can be both a bane and a blessing. Some congregations do a fine job of maintaining the parsonage, treating it as the private home of the minister's family. In such cases there is freedom from dealing with some of the stresses of home ownership. Other congregations, however, treat the parsonage as an extension of the church, and feel free to drop in at will. Stories abound of parishioners who walk in without knocking. It is not unheard of in smaller churches to have the church office, complete with the mimeograph machine, in the parsonage, with people coming and going at all hours. This lack of privacy in one's home is obviously a source of stress. Some find that getting necessary repairs done in the parsonage means hounding a property committee, an awkward and embarrassing process at best. Since it is the wife who is in the home the most, she is the one who often finds this most stressful.

5) Feeling Disenfranchised

For those wives (or husbands of clergy) who have a real commitment to the church and ministry, there is another frustration. They find themselves intimately involved in an institution that expects that they play an active role, but affords them no power within the system.

> A clergy wife is expected never to take a stand on controversial issues, never to run for public office in the church, to dress properly and to be silent—or, as Carolyn Taylor Gutierrez has put it, to be a 'holy noodlehead.' She must remain active, involved and friendly in a highly politicized social system without being seen as having overt political power (Oswald, Gutierrez, and Dean, 1980. p. 14).

To have the spouse active in a significant role within the church is often seen as a conflict of interest. This was a high stressor for me in the early years of our marriage. I felt just as strongly called to ministry as my husband did. Our family circumstances did not allow me a professional ministerial career at that time. Though I found some significant ways to use my talents and my calling, I felt that the major channel open to me to effect change within the church was through my husband. It is a small miracle that our marriage survived, as I repeatedly greeted my weary husband at the end of the day with a whole long list of great ideas for things that could be done in the church. It was a frustration to me that I had no power to work on these changes except through him.

6) Serving as a Go-between

How to keep out of the middle between their husbands and the parishioners is one of the key things clergy wives (and husbands) need to learn. Parishioners often find it easier to talk to the spouse than to the clergyperson, especially if they have a complaint about some aspect of church life, or have something they think the minister should be doing. For the spouse to be the "message-taker," especially when the message is bad news or requires something more for the minister to do often places a strain on the spouse and the marriage.

7) Employment, Insecurity and Relocation

Clergy wives are very vulnerable to the success or failure of their husbands' jobs. As one woman put it: "Our whole life style is tied up in how things are going in the parish." To some extent this is true for other families in our society as well. There is always the risk that the husband will lose a job, resulting in relocation, uprooting families, and the wife having to give up her job. However, for most non-clergy couples there is the *possibility*, at least, of the husband finding a position within the same geographic locality. But for clergy families, job loss means getting out of the parsonage, and almost always relocation to a distant community, requiring major changes for the whole family. As one wife said: "If someone comes to the house yelling about something my husband did, or my husband is taking an unpopular stand on an issue, or there is conflict in the church, we absorb it and wonder if he is going to lose his job over this one."

8) Who Is My Pastor?

There is no way that a clergyperson can or should be both a spouse *and* a pastor or counselor to his/her marital partner. As one clergyman said: "I know, I tried!" Some, but not all, spouses keenly feel the lack of having a pastor to turn to in their times of personal and spiritual need. For example, if a clergy spouse is "spiritually dry," to whom can she turn? As you will see in the data (Appendices V & VIII), spouses often feel they have no one to go to on this issue. One wife said, "I used to turn to my pastor for help when I needed it. Then I married a minister. My husband ministers to everyone, but who is there for me?" Then she added, "I can't afford a counselor." Furthermore, there seems to be an assumption by some that if one is married to a pastor then no further help should be needed. One wife told of being at a large hospital during the time her son was dying. She desperately needed someone to talk to besides her husband. A social worker came to see her, and as soon as she learned that this mother was married to a minister the social worker said, "Then you won't be needing me."

Some wives also spoke of the fact that in spiritual growth or Bible study groups within the church, people often turn to them expecting they have the answers simply by virtue of their being married to the minister. These spouses feel it is unacceptable for them to share their doubts or lack of knowledge, and hence do not find these groups nurturing to their personal spiritual journeys.

9) Limelight or Anonymity

Finally, two groups of spouses spoke about facets of being a "minister's wife" that on the surface seem quite contradictory. Some spoke of always feeling in the limelight. Others spoke of feeling as if they were treated as an invisible appendage, often being ignored when they were with their husbands. Underneath both of these comments, I believe, is the issue of their wanting to seen as a normal individual, not simply as the "minister's wife."

10) Stresses on Male Spouses

"They don't know how to deal with someone in my position," said one male spouse. That about sums up the current role-expectation of the male spouse of a female parish minister. There seem to be few expectations from the churches for this relatively new role. Perhaps even more important, the male spouse comes with few, if any, *internal* expectations about what his role should be. Most already have established their own identity and career, which helps them be seen as totally separate individuals. Yet some are experiencing a little of the anonymity that wives have experienced, when they are introduced with "this is our minister's husband," or occasionally even, "this is our minister's *wife!*" The male spouses I spoke with also indicated that they would not want or feel free to assume any leadership role in a church where their wives are pastors. They too feel like disenfranchised members of the congregation with no pastor or place to participate at meaningful levels.

A more in-depth study of male spouses of clergy may be found in the Alban publication, *Men Married to Ministers*, by Laura Deming and Jack Stubbs.

C. Stresses on Clergy Marriages

In spite of the stresses, clergy and their spouses seemed to agree that the pluses outweighed the minuses. Many spoke of the sense of meaning and purpose that comes from ministry, the rich mix of people they get to know, both in the church and in the larger community and the many ways they were able to share the ministry with each other. Yet, in the midst of these pluses there are some difficult stresses on marriages that come as a result of the clergy role. Since marriage is not easy, even under the best of circumstances, it is important to note where the extra stresses are on clergy marriages, and to find ways to deal with them. Several of the following stress factors are similar to the ones mentioned for clergy and spouses individually, but I address them here because of their special impact on clergy marriages.

1) Expectations

David and Vera Mace (1980), who have done one of the most recent in-depth studies on clergy marriages, found that 85% of the clergy couples said they felt their marriage was expected to be a model of perfection. They found that, "Clergy couples are almost obsessed with the feeling that they are expected to be superhuman and to provide models for the congregation and community" (p. 41). In another study, Sawin and Whybrew (1985) note that "Protestants consider their minister's personal and family life as 'tools for ministry.' Unfortunately, family modeling is often measured by moralistic 'thou shalt nots' of public behavior rather than by how families handle deeper issues" (p. 2). These expectations are felt by many of the couples I talked with, though *not* as strongly as these two studies seem to indicate. However, to the degree that couples feel this expectation, resistance is created toward couples getting help, or even toward dealing realistically with needed growth points in their marriages. If clergy couples are trying to live out other people's expectations of a perfect marriage, it is hard for them to deal with their own real marriage. It leads them into a game of "let's pretend." As one Conference Minister said, "Congregations desperately need clergy marriages to work. They think that if their ministers can't make it work, how can *they?* That's an awful burden!" Also it is even more painful and stressful when the couple is aware that they are falling far short of these expectations.

2) Couple and Family Time

Sawin and Whybrew (1985) write that:

> A double bind is produced when the church defines its work as
> "God's work" and its pastors as God's agents. The church speaks
> with prophetic voice to most breadwinners (through preaching
> and pastoral intervention) challenging them not to be workahol-
> ics and neglect their family relationships. The church's own
> leaders however, are encouraged to put work first and are re-
> warded for being omnipresent and giving of themselves "self-
> lessly" whenever called upon. It is most difficult for a family to
> put mundane daily needs ahead of such a "calling" (p. 3).

If the church is the primary responsibility and marriage secondary,
the spouse of a parish minister is up against a very powerful rival.

Attentiveness and good listening are at the heart of what fosters
a healthy marriage. Clergypersons (as well as other helping professions) often come home exhausted from listening to other people
and ministering to their needs and therefore are unable to listen.
They are too drained to be fully present to their spouses. Too little
time together and poor communication can take their toll on a marriage.

3) Changing Roles

Our whole society is experiencing the impact of changing roles of
men and women. There is renegotiating taking place around responsibilities of home and family. This is presenting new possibilities for sharing and rounding out the life dimensions of both men
and women. A number of the clergy couples I interviewed are seeking to share home and child care as well as the "bread-winning"
role. These couples seem to find the flexibility of the clergy schedule a plus, but the unpredictability and time demands of the job are
complicating factors.

I believe these changes will have an additional impact. Roy Oswald of the Alban Institute finds that male clergy turn to their
spouses for support more than men in other occupations. My study
confirms that wives are the major and *sometimes sole confidantes*
for their clergy husbands. I question how the time and energy demands of two-career marriages will affect this key support system
for male clergy? How will it affect the marriages? Will this leave
male clergy with a real deficit in support or will it be the impetus
for broadening their support-networks? The changes taking place in
this area are bound to be stressful even if they lead to something
good.

D. . . . And No Place To Blow?

Both clergy and spouses of clergy overwhelmingly indicated that it was difficult to find persons to talk to about personal issues and that they were hesitant to ask for help when they needed it. (See Appendix III) Why is this? Using the words of the people I interviewed, here are some clues:

> I don't have many friends. I'm so busy that I don't have time for people outside the parish.

> I wouldn't talk with parishioners. I don't want them to see my blemishes—at least not all of them.

> If I acknowledge to others certain needs of mine, then I'm worried about confidentiality and especially how this would reflect on my clergy husband.

> It's hard work to go and find help. It's just easier to manage the pain.

> There is a basic hesitation for ministers to seek help. We think we're exempt because we are help-givers not help-receivers.

> I rarely share or seek support. Part of that is my nature. When I hurt I want to be alone.

> I might share with a couple of carefully chosen clergy, but I don't trust most clergy to keep confidences. I've been burned too often.

> We don't have the money to get the counseling we could use.

> I wouldn't talk about personal issues with Conference people, because it might influence future employment opportunities.

> Most clergy groups are too competitive and seldom do we share at any deep levels.

> It's difficult to share personal issues unless you have already developed a strong, trusting personal relationship with someone. I seldom have time for these kinds of relationships.

> I feel like I always have to screen what I say. If I have a friend in the parish there are subjects that are off limits. I can't talk about many church issues, my husband or our marriage.

> I'm an alcoholic in private. I found one friend who is in the parish who is struggling with this, but I'm not sure where else to go.

My husband believes that I should be strong and work things out for myself. He's resistant to me seeing a counselor.

It's hard for me to talk with people or seek support. It has to do with my perception of myself. I'm a care-giver and not necessarily a care-receiver. I am one who has the gift to be strong.

The role sets you apart. People treat clergy like they have lots of answers to emotional problems and believe they ought to have enough spiritual resources so they don't need people.

There is something about being a care-giver that makes it easier to listen to other people's problems than to share my own.

If as a helper I need help, then what kind of a helper am I?

We live in a fishbowl in a small town. I'm afraid of saying something that will be fuel for the fire.

If I'm a mature competent person, I shouldn't need to ask for help. It would be an admission that I don't have my act together.

When I try to share my issues or problems with some parishioners, their eyes glaze over. They seem to expect me to listen endlessly to their concerns, but not have any of my own.

Our congregations want to put us on pedestals. They think we shouldn't have our ups and downs. If we tell them, it threatens them. It's because of an unrealistic view of the ministry. It drives me crazy, but it also makes me pull back.

However, some clergy and spouses present a different picture. Their stories describe good support systems. These persons often acknowledged some of the same feelings and limitations of the clergy role, yet they indicated that they had good support. Here's what they said:

I have shared my vulnerability in a prayer group. I've told them I'm spiritually dry and they have prayed for me. Part of this was a conscious modeling on my part. There is some control about what I will share. But every time I give them a crack at it they come through with all sorts of love and warmth.

I had a classic case of burn-out with incredible pain. I shared it with a Catholic friend of mine and got a referral for counseling. I shared it with the Deacons. They responded supportively.

The support has been there when I needed it—or I went out and found it. My wife, my colleagues, the Area Minister, my studies, journal work have been important supports.

Finding support has not been a problem for me. There is a local group of clergy wives, my family who is close by, a counselor and the Area Minister have all been helpful.

As a clergyperson just starting out, I chose to join a multiple staff. Some of the members were very supportive, especially through those first years in ministry. My wife, key lay people and a counselor are also very helpful.

Life experiences forced me to get help. Now I live with the knowledge that there is help and I know how to find it. A support group and other relationships keep me going. I'm less lonely now.

My own style is not to keep things in. I'm a risk-taker and share vulnerability. I have lots of friends, both clergy and lay. Obviously, I share different things with different people.

A support group of clergy couples is very important to us. We need close friends we can be open with.

We deliberately seek out friends who are not a part of the parish. Then we take time to nourish these friendships.

I would not be without a support group of trusted peers.

I feel fortunate that I have a number of people who are supportive. When my wife was very sick, we sought out the chaplain in the hospital. He became a close friend. We are free enough to lovingly confront each other, share joys and pains and think out loud together.

I develop my real support systems with the people I work with and it helps that it's away from my husband's job and the church.

Centering prayer is a major resource for me. The payoffs in how I approach the rest of life are tremendous.

Such variety! We could simply conclude that there are no clear norms for how clergy or clergy spouses get support. Some people reach out for support and some don't. Yet, in the midst of all this diversity there seem to be some underlying issues which determine whether people build support systems or not. We'll look at some of these issues in the chapters that deal with the underlying stumbling blocks to getting support. First, however, let us consider whether all people really *need* support?

CHAPTER III

Support: Who Needs It?

Clergy experience in their own lives the brokenness and pain of the human condition, which is often contrary to the expectations of the Church, culture and self. This alienation creates crises of various forms, guises and degrees. (*Resolution on Clergy in Crisis*, Fourteenth General Synod of the United Church of Christ, 1983)

There is a definite need for support for clergy and their spouses. My husband is available to so many people and at no cost. Who is available to us? (Wife of a clergyman)

For each of us the point is how to live with dignity and fullness despite the pain and changes life brings. Without people to share it with, without courage to be vulnerable, and without compassion, life is empty. (John C. Harris, 1982, p. 149).

Interest in support systems or support groups is a relatively modern phenomenon. Perhaps the mobility of our times and the resultant loss of the extended family has left us with fewer built-in support systems than people had in the past. Instead, we now have support groups for people going through illness, bereavement, divorce, or any number of other experiences. And there has been an explosive growth in psychotherapy and peer counseling, and the beginnings of a reaffirmation of spiritual guidance. To what extent is this focus on supportive relationships the result of the increased stress of our times, and to what extent is it due to a new understanding of a basic human need? Whatever the cause, there is an impressive amount of data that points to the need for support.

There have been several studies that validate the conclusion that support systems are crucial in facing life crises. Eric Lindemann, for example, who did the now-famous study of the survivors of the Cocoanut Grove fire which killed 491 people, found two kinds of survivors: 1) those who recovered quickly and well after the fire, and often had an even higher level of well-being after recovery than before; 2) those who did not recover well and whose well-being did not measure up to what it had been prior to the disaster. The *key difference between these two groups, he concluded, was the quality of their support systems.*

It merely had to do with the quantity of people who checked into a person's life over a period of time. If individuals had a significant number of people checking in with them just to see how they were or give them emotional support, that constituted a high quality support system. In contrast, those who did not have that kind of support system had a long and painful recovery (Oswald, 1981, p. 5).

I can testify to the importance of this kind of support when we went through a major loss in our own family. When our son died after a long illness, we were surrounded by support from our congregation, family and friends. This significantly facilitated our healing. Yet I wonder what it would have been like if our pain had been of a type that is not so easily shared? For instance, what if our pain had been caused by a son who was on drugs, or a daughter in prison, or a marriage falling apart? Where would the support have come from then?

Anton Antonovsky, an Israeli professor of medical sociology at Ben Gurion University, did a nine-year study of 7000 persons in California. His data show that "people with many social ties, such as marriage, close friendships, extended families, church membership and other group associations, have far lower mortality." (Oswald, 1981, p. 5) This study provides a powerful connection between support systems and life expectancy.

To apply this more specifically to research done with clergy, a study done by Mills and Koval (1971) found that clergy who had "no sources of support beyond themselves reported fewer successful outcomes in the succeeding period. It seemed that *stress was hardest to resolve when external support was absent.* (my emphasis) This was particularly true when the source of stress was in marriage or family" (p. 32). Those clergy who had good supports handled their stress better in at least 20% of the stress situations.

Gail Sheehy's study (1981, p. 164) confirms that people with a sense of well-being enjoy twice as many close friends as the average person, and that these friends are a front line of defense in the hard times.

If good support simply consisted of the quantity of people checking into a person's life in the midst of a crisis, as suggested by Lindemann, then clergy families may have some of the best support

systems. Some congregations are superb at being supportive when
there is a death or an illness in the clergy's family. However, support is needed in more than these public and easily understood
crises times. Support is more than people "checking in" with the
person who is hurting.

The studies mentioned above bolster our assumption that everyone has basic need for support. But what do we mean by support?
Support comes in many forms. Carol Pierce and Marian Coger
(1985 p. 26) suggest a number of words which describe support.
Pierce proposes the "Three C's" as basics: Comfort, Clarification,
Confrontation. We need people whom we can trust with our pain
and uncertainty and who will *comfort* us, often by just being good
listeners. We need people who help us *clarify* by asking the right
questions and pointing us to significant resources. We need people
who care about us enough to lovingly *confront* us with that which
we don't see or have been avoiding. Coger adds two more "C's":
Collaborators and Clowns. We need people to work with who have
some of the same goals, visions and problems we do, and who
therefore, can be *collaborators* (or colleagues) and help us avoid
isolation and stagnation in ministry. *Clowns* are persons who can
add perspective and support through humor or a light touch at an
appropriate moment. A friend of mine adds *celebrators* to the list.
We need people who will celebrate our triumphs, large or small,
and affirm us as persons. No one person or group can meet all our
support needs. Whenever our support network is too narrowly defined we are at risk. Who are the people in your personal and
professional life who act as comforters, clarifiers, confronters, collaborators, clowns and celebrators?

If the *quality* and *breadth* of support is a major factor in our
ability to withstand change and stress of any kind, then it is important to have a support network in place. The worst time to try to
build a support network is in the midst of crisis, when there is so
little time and energy for anything extra. Furthermore, support is
not only for times of crisis. Regular contact with supportive people
is often what helps us keep our perspective and, in some instances,
helps avoid the crisis.

Many of the people who responded to my questionnaire (See
Appendices IV-VIII) said their major support was God. ("My help
cometh from the Lord.") Mills and Koval's data indicate that clergy
who have a strong sense of spiritual support rarely report aloneness
when the stress is high (1971 p. 31). Most of us can affirm that
there are times when we know this divine reality and support in
our deepest being. Yet some of the clergy and spouses I talked with
indicated that they hunger for more connectedness with God. Many

indicated they struggle to find the time to nurture the spiritual dimensions of their lives. Finding the ways to tap into God's support as a major source of comfort, clarification and confrontation is essential to our well-being and our ministry.

Personal support and spiritual support are both needed. Some people believe that clergy and their spouses should have so much faith in God that they should not need other kinds of support. In my interviews I asked clergy and their spouses if they felt their faith in God meant that they needed less support from people. Their response was an emphatic "No"! While affirming that "God is a very present help," most also affirmed their need for people. In fact, many believed that one of the most important ways God comes to them is through people. This is good incarnational theology. After all, it is in the person of Jesus that God has come to us most fully. And God has called us into community and encourages us to "bear one another's burdens, and so fulfill the law of Christ" (Galatians 6:2). Thus we are encouraged to be channels for God's support to each other.

Even though we can conclude that support is essential for all of us, my research indicates that clergy and clergy spouses often have quite sparse support systems. I echo Roy Oswald's puzzlement over why so few clergy take time to build support.

> . . . it is hard to understand why so little effort seems to go into creating support systems. As I travel around the country and interact with clergy, I encounter very few who see this as an important ingredient in their professional well-being and competence. Most see support systems as a kind of luxury—if you have a good one, you're lucky and if you don't—that's tough. They are not fully aware of how vulnerable they are, and how much more competent and effective they might be if they took time to develop a solid support network for themselves in an intentional way (1981, p. 6).

This brings us to the heart of my study. *If support is so essential, what keeps so many clergy and spouses from building these networks?*

CHAPTER IV

Underlying Stumbling Blocks to Getting Support: Cultural and Sexual Scripts

As I listened to people tell their stories it became clear that there are some underlying factors behind the difficulty clergy and their spouses have in finding people to talk with about personal issues. Attitudes and beliefs often become the major stumbling blocks to getting the support they need. I will be describing several of these blocks in the next three chapters. The following quotes help us move into considering the first of these stumbling blocks: cultural and sexual scripts.

> I'm something of a loner." (A clergyman)

> I don't want to ask for help. I'm a guarded person. I don't know where this is rooted, but it came before the clergy role. (A clergyman)

> Isolation in ministry may be more of a cultural and male issue than a clergy one." (A clergyman)

> We may use ministry to get in touch with people without having to get close. (A Conference Minister)

> Often all we tell each other are the things we are sure we can't get criticized for. Everyone of us needs love from each other and none of us is willing to tell about the pain that needs the love. (A clergyman talking about clergy gatherings)

Hypothesis: Underlying the hesitancy to ask for help are both a cultural and a sexual script. These scripts tend to lock people into a position of independence and self-sufficency rather than allowing them to move on to interdependence.

Early influences lead all of us to make decisions about how we should behave and how we will view our world. These decisions form the scripts for our lives. They continue to shape how we act and how we relate to others, *unless* they are re-decided (Steiner, 1974).

Individualism, independence and self-sufficiency are particularly strong values in our American culture. They provide an ideal and a foundation for many people's scripts. Robert Bellah and his co-authors, in their book, *Habits of the Heart* (1985), have made a significant contribution to our understanding of individualism and commitment in America. We get some understanding of how this cultural ideal shapes our view of life by looking at Bellah's description of the "American hero:"

> America is the inventor of that most mythic hero, the cowboy, who again and again saves a society he can never completely fit into. The cowboy has a special talent—he can shoot faster and straighter than most other men—and a special sense of justice. But these characteristics make him so unique that he can never fully belong to society. It is as if the myth says you can be a truly good person, worthy of admiration and love, only if you resist fully joining the group.... The connection of moral courage and lonely individualism is even tighter for that other more modern American hero, the hard-boiled detective. From Sam Spade to Serpico, the detective is a loner. He is often unsuccessful in conventional terms, working out of a shabby office where the phone never rings. But his marginality is also his strength. When the detective begins his quest, it appears to be an isolated incident. But as it develops, the case turns out to be linked to the powerful and privileged of the community. Society, particularly "high society" is corrupt to the core. To seek justice in a corrupt society, the American detective must be tough, and above all, he must be a loner (p. 145).

> Both the cowboy and the hard-boiled detective tell us something important about American individualism. The cowboy, like the detective, can be valuable to society only because he is a completely autonomous individual who stands outside it. To serve society, one must be able to stand alone, not needing others, not depending on their judgment, and not submitting to their wishes. Yet this individualism is not selfishness. Indeed, it is a kind of heroic selflessness. One accepts the necessity of remaining alone in order to serve the values of the group. Yet it is part of the profound ambiguity of the mythology of American individualism that its moral heroism is always just a step away from despair. (p. 146)

I was struck by how closely several of these descriptive phrases were echoed in my interviews. For example:

Clergyperson—"I'm neither fish nor fowl. People see me as different and sometimes I feel different."
Bellah—"... his characteristics make him so unique that he can never fully belong to society"

Clergyperson—"People put me on a pedestal. I need to be something special for them." "It's hard to be part of their social group."
Bellah—I "can only be a truly good person worthy of admiration and love if I resist joining the group."

Clergyperson—"The role opens doors for me that I won't discount. What I represent to people is important."
Bellah—"... his marginality is also his strength."

Clergyperson—"I can't really be their close friend and their pastor too."
Bellah—She/he "accepts the necessity of remaining alone in order to serve the values of the group."

Clergyperson—"It's very lonely to be set apart."
Bellah—"... moral heroism is just a step away from despair."

There are two ways that this American script impinges on the lives of clergy and their spouses. First, clergy and their spouses often unconsciously live out the isolated, "lone ranger" script as part of their personal view of life. After all, clergy and their spouses are very much part of the culture in which they live, so it is natural that many would be affected by a dominant cultural script. Often, in my interviews with male clergy I heard, "I see myself as something of a loner." In some, this seemed to be coupled with an attitude of "this is the way it has to be for me in my position." Yet, I sensed that this had more to do with a learned cultural script than the limitation of the clergy position. One clergyman said this quite clearly: "I don't want to ask for help. I don't know where it is rooted, but it came before the clergy role."

The second way this popular, self-sufficient, lone-ranger model can affect clergy is that there will be constant pressure and expectation from parishioners for clergy to function in this independent mode. Some people will be more likely to admire clergy if they operate this way, and may consider them weak if they aren't self-sufficient, authoritative, "take charge," leaders. This script pattern can permeate church staffs also. For example, a clergywoman who adopted a collegial style in a multiple staff situation was perceived as a weak leader, and was given little credibility until she changed her style of operating to an independent and autonomous one. Only then was she seen as being a strong and effective leader.

I'm not suggesting that independence and self-sufficiency are
negative traits. I am suggesting that taken as ends or ideals they fall
short of both the human and the Christian concept of wholeness
and maturity. As I observe people's life journeys toward maturity, it
strikes me that we move through a developmental process that pro-
gresses in this fashion:

Dependence→Anti-dependence→Independence→Interdependence

We begin life as children, totally dependent. Then in adolescence
we go through a time of being very resistant (anti-dependent) toward those upon whom we have depended. As we mature into
adulthood, we become more independent and self-sufficient, making our own decisions and developing our own identity. Finally, we
can begin to recognize how *inter*dependent we all are, and begin to
live more in relationship and community. Obviously, this is not just
a once-in-a-lifetime progression. We may cycle through these various stages in many relationships and situations throughout life.
However, *it is my contention that the American script pattern encourages us to idealize independence and stop there, with little encouragement to move on to interdependence.* Many studies find this
especially true for males, though I see it becoming true for many
females as they seek to succeed in a male-oriented society. In the
past, the female cultural script often encouraged women to stop at
the *dependent* position. The women's movement has encouraged
many to move on to an independent stance, but it runs the same
risk of locking women in to the cultural script that has been more
prevalent for males. In a culture that sees independence as the goal,
one may fear that dependence of any kind might be a step back-
wards into an earlier symbiotic dependent relationship of childhood.

Interdependence is clearly not symbiotic. Rather it means that
persons who can function well independently will allow times to
have their needs for support and dependence met, and will be able
to meet other people's needs for this as well. To the extent that
clergy and their spouses get stalled in their development by the cultural script that idealizes independence, they may be cut off from
finding support.

Furthermore, independence as the goal is not faithful to a Biblical model of ministry or our theology. Jesus himself was not a
loner. There were times when he sought aloneness, but that is quite
different than being a loner. His style of ministry was to surround
himself with the fellowship of disciples, and he called them friends
(John 15:15). The word "friend" has an inherent interdependent

quality. When the disciples went out to minister and perform miracles in his name, Jesus sent them in pairs. Here is a model of companionship and collegiality in ministry.

Perhaps the most powerful recognition of our interdependence comes from Paul's declaration of our interconnectedness with each other. Our Biblical faith talks about "mature manhood" (personhood) as being attained by using our gifts to build up the body of Christ "until we all attain the unity of the faith and the knowledge of the Son of God" (Ephesians 4:12-13). And in Romans 12:4-5 Paul says, "For as in one body we have many members, and all the members do not have the same function, so we, though many, are one body in Christ, and individually members one of another" (Romans 12:4-5). The Christian lifestyle is one of community and interdependence. Again, Paul writes to the church at Rome saying that he wanted to visit them so that they could be "mutually encouraged by each other's faith" (Romans 1:12). Thus, I maintain that the American cultural script of individualism and independence is in conflict with a faith that upholds the ideal of interdependence and community.

The second sexual script is a more specific version of this cultural one, because it applies especially to males in our society. Carol Gilligan, in her book, *In a Different Voice* (1982), helps us look more closely at male/female differences and how they might influence our support systems. She sees differences between male and female patterning in our society stemming from the fact that boys are encouraged to separate from their mothers, while girls, being of the same sex as their mothers, are encouraged to continue in relationship. She quotes Nancy Chodorow's study which found that, as a result of these early care patterns:

> ... masculinity is defined through separation while femininity is defined through attachment. Male gender identity is threatened by intimacy while female gender identity is threatened by separation. Thus males have difficulty with relationships, while females tend to have problems with individuation. (p. 8)

This has serious ramifications regarding support systems for men. If men shy away from intimacy, they cut themselves off from the most meaningful source of support. These findings are corroborated by many other studies. For example Daniel Levinson in his book, *Seasons of a Man's Life*, concluded:

> In our interviews, friendship was largely noticeable by its absence. As a tentative generalization, we would say that close

friendship with a man or woman is rarely experienced by American men.

McClelland (1975, p. 85-86) stated that:

Women are more concerned with both sides of an interdependent relationship and are quicker to recognize their interdependence.

Erikson's studies of Luther and Gandhi echo what I heard from the female spouses of several clergy. Speaking of Luther and Gandhi, he says that

while the relationship between self and society is achieved in magnificent articulation, both men are compromised in their capacity for intimacy and live at great personal distance from others. Thus Luther in his devotion to Faith, like Gandhi in his devotion to Truth, ignore the people most closely around them while working instead toward the glory of God. (Gilligan, p. 155)

Gilligan goes on to conclude:

The stereotypes suggest a splitting of love and work that relegates expressive capacities to woman while placing instrumental abilities in the masculine domain. Yet looked at from a different perspective, these stereotypes reflect a conception of adulthood that itself is out of balance, favoring separateness of the individual self over connection to others, and leaning more toward an autonomous life of work than toward interdependence of love and care (p. 17).

The underlying epistemology is more the Greek ideal of knowledge as correspondence between mind and form than the Biblical conception of knowing as a process of human relationship (p. 173).

Gail Sheehy in *Pathfinders* (1981) says that men can seldom trust other men "with admission of naivete, failure, fears or even the disclosure of a man's bluntest ambitions" (p. 166). Therefore, she concludes that man-to-man friendships are more instrumental than emotional. It seems that women have an easier time of friendships because of their earlier patterning and because there has been more permission in our society for women to be interdependent.

My research verified that these script patterns are significant issues for clergy and clergy spouses when it comes to gaining support. One clergyman described the inner conflict that this creates for him:

> It's difficult to ask for help because of my nature. I don't like to admit weakness. I don't like to be vulnerable. I was brought up with the superman mentality. I'm supposed to be superman. My theology tells me "no", that's not right. Jesus was the epitome of powerlessness and in that way was most powerful. My theology breaks down, because I don't want people to see that I am a hurting person.

Another clergyman, who has done some studies regarding clergy and male/female differences, put it this way: "There is a whole constellation of drives, feelings and needs for male clergy that mean disaster. We're a bunch of wounded, out-of-touch, dry people, who have lots of gifts and want to use them, who want to open up and be re-empowered." His findings also concluded that female clergy, for the most part, give some priority to their relationships. "They know if they are married that it takes time to nurture this commitment. A lot of men don't know this," he said. "We talk about quality-time with our spouse and families and fool ourselves."

This script pattern is often evident in clergy groups. In my interviews, a significant number of male clergy spoke about how clergy gatherings tended to be more competitive than truly collegial and supportive. They experienced an unwillingness to trust or share feelings with each other. They feared that their colleagues would not respect confidentiality. Even when they did trust, it appears that it was sometimes difficult to respond fully to each other. During the time our son was dying, my husband shared his pain with fellow clergy at a "support day." The group listened, but only one person spoke to him about it after the meeting. It was a curious and disconcerting silence, and might have been devastating if he had not had good support elsewhere. I had a similar experience with a clergy colleague group (which happened to be all males except for myself). After learning that I had cancer, I told them about it and my fear. They listened, but most were unable to respond in any way that helped me feel heard or cared about.

These script patterns are also confirmed by my questionnaire, which reveals that male clergy rely mainly on their spouses and God for support (Appendix VI). Female clergy, on the other hand, have a wider network of support systems (Appendix VII). More often than the males, the female clergy spoke of support systems as an absolute necessity for them.

However, the theory that females have better support networks than males seems to break down when we look at the data that comes from the female spouses (Appendix VIII). Many clergy wives do not have the same breadth in their support systems as the female clergy. Clergy wives, more than any of the other groups studied, indicated that they had "no one" with whom to talk over certain issues. My impression from the interviews is that a number of wives were the primary absorbers of their husbands' problems, but had fewer places to go with their own. Loyalty to their primary marriage relationship, the limitations placed on sharing due to their husband's role, and the lack of female "colleagues" gave them fewer outlets or sources of support. Those wives who are employed outside the home and outside of the community seem to have an easier time building good support systems. On the basis of this data, I conclude that clergy wives (especially those in the more traditional role) are often cut off from good interdependent relationships by their role.

Obviously, not all the people I interviewed fit these script patterns. Some spoke about patterns in their lives that seemed very interdependent. There were male clergy who were very willing to ask for help and to share openly. And there were some men who dealt more freely with their feelings and needs than some of the women. However, these cultural and sexual scripts are prevalent enough that they must be dealt with when trying to unblock that which inhibits many clergy and spouses from finding support.

If breaking free of these scripts is crucial to living more interdependent, supported lives then it is important to identify what enables this kind of change to happen. Carl Rogers maintains that we are most open to change when we are hurting badly enough, or are bored enough with our lives the way they are, or are exposed to someone who shows us the possibilities of a better way. From talking with the clergy and spouses who live more interdependent lifestyles it is clear that they came to this in a variety of ways. A few grew up in homes that modeled and nurtured an interdependent lifestyle. For some it developed gradually through therapy or life experience. Some were bored or dissatisfied with life and observed a better way modelled by persons they respected. For instance, several clergy spoke of being in a group where a respected colleague risked being open, revealing pain and vulnerability. They observed that this helped rather than hindered them as persons and ministers. They noted that they gained rather than lost respect for the persons who were willing to share openly. One person put it this way:

> You may not even know you need a support system unless you have had one, and learned of its possibilities. For me it began

with the experience of a Shalom Retreat that was offered by the Massachusetts Conference of the UCC. People there risked sharing vulnerability and we all grew in the process.

Breaking out of these kinds of scripts also can happen more dramatically through personal crisis or a religious experience. In fact, the catalyst for change which was mentioned most frequently in my interviews was that of personal crisis. Here are excerpts from the stories of turning points in four clergymen's lives.

Before my wife's illness, I didn't have people I could turn to. Her illness was a very painful and humbling experience. I learned a lot about my own needs. Before the illness I had a John Wayne approach to life.

As a young person I learned male competition and never allowed male intimacy. Finally, when I was confronted with having to work out my relationship with my father, I learned I had to forgive him. After that happened I was able to have close relationships with men. This also enhanced my relationships with women. I used women less to take care of me. They became people rather than "mother substitutes." So, I am not lonely in ministry. I have good friendships with people in my churches and with my clergy peers.

I was frightened about my ministry. I didn't see how I could stay in it another 20 years, and I didn't know what else to do. I didn't understand my problem, or that help was available. I was nervous about going to a psychiatrist because I still thought they were for sick people. I met a minister who was sensitive, and in desperation I talked with him. He saw my feelings of trappedness in larger, mid-life terms of individuation and got me into therapy with a Jungian therapist. That opened up a rich growthexperience, an inner spiritual journey, and more interpersonal relations. Before that it was like being thirsty, but not knowing that there was water. Now years later, I'm in a clergy supportgroup and see a counselor/spiritual guide. I keep this going, not because I'm desperate, but because it keeps me growing.

At one time I had no resources. When coping with my wife's alcohol problem, I got into Al-anon, which was a great support. I learned that support is not only valuable, but essential for me.

Crisis propelled each of these individuals out of their independent, self-sufficient script into interdependence and more intimate human relationships. A deeper, richer, more authentic way of living was the gift that came out of the crisis times.

The American independent, self-sufficient script is a religious issue as well as a psychological one. It may block us from a trusting, dependent or interdependent relationship with God. Several of the persons I interviewed spoke of religious experiences during their crises. In the midst of crisis they discovered God and the support of people in some new ways. It is difficult to identify which came first! How much does our American ideal of self-sufficiency and independence cut us off from God as well as from other people? Though my questionnaire data (Appendix IV) indicates that male clergy turn to God as one of their primary sources of support, it is also interesting to note that "spiritual dryness" is *the* issue that tops the list of personal issues for male clergy. Interestingly, it seems to be a somewhat less significant issue for female clergy (Appendix VII). This suggests that persons who know that they cannot do it alone are more likely to be open to God *and* other people.

CHAPTER V

Underlying Stumbling Blocks to Getting Support: Metaphors for Ministry

People want us to be spiritual, and to be right. They want us to be for them what they need. Part of us gets sucked into wanting to be perceived this way. To seek help for ourselves means to blow our cover or confront others with the fact that we aren't all they want. But if our concern is to be honest and forthright, we have to deal with that. If we hide behind the role expectations and projected needs, then it is hard to go after the resources that are available and it's hard to ask for help. (A clergyman)

There needs to be a whole different way of looking at being a parish minister. It just doesn't seem to be o.k. to be human and vulnerable if you are a clergyperson. We hate the stereotype, but we buy into it. We can't let our guard down. Why wouldn't we have issues? We're all making our way. (A clergywoman)

All of us want to find God in our midst, so we try to elevate certain persons to godlike status to satisfy the myth within us. It doesn't work. By setting up our own gods, be they clergy or not, we only ask for disillusionment. (Clyde Reid, 1974, p.44)

Ordination to the Christian Ministry does not transport any person into another category of human experience. Needs, emotions, feelings remain the same. The basic dishonesty of Christian ministry today is that many of us have been programmed into pretending that we are different than ordinary mortals, and many members of our congregations play that game so that they can live vicariously through us. (Harold Frey, *The Pain and Joy of Ministry*)

The most dangerous expectations are the ones we put on ourselves. (A clergyperson)

There is nothing more holy than being human. (A clergyperson)

You must give birth to your images. They are the future waiting to be born. (Rainer Maria Rilke, *Letters to a Young Poet*, letter #3)

Hypothesis: The way one views the ministerial role is a key issue in whether clergy and their spouses are able to get the support they need.

How do we describe the ministerial role? What metaphors do we use? Metaphors, (those words or images we use to describe our ministries) are significant indicators of how we see ourselves. Furthermore, how we see ourselves as ministers is one of the key issues in whether or not we acknowledge our own needs, and get, or fail to get, support. In my interviews with clergy, and also with spouses who are involved in the ministry, the metaphors they used most often to describe themselves were "caregiver" and "helper." Several clergy used the Biblical image of "shepherd," which is also a caregiver role. Clearly, caregiving is a function of parish ministry. It is one of the most common expectations congregations have of their ministers.

Let's look at some of the implications of seeing oneself as *the helper* or *the caregiver* or *the shepherd of the flock*. As individuals talked about themselves, it was clear that these images or metaphors implied *giving* rather than *receiving*. Often there is a hidden assumption made by the clergyperson and the congregation that caregiving is a one-way street. There is a person (the minister, the helper) who has something to give; and there are some people who need what he or she has to give (the "helpee," the one in need of care, the sheep of the flock). Though most of us would not philosophically defend this "one-way street" concept, it is almost inevitable that we get trapped by it. To the extent that we do fall into it, we cut ourselves off from realizing that we too need support or help. We get lured into believing or pretending that we are the ones who "have it all together" for others to come to for help. Several clergypersons put it quite clearly: "If I am a helper and I need help, what kind of a helper am I?" Or another, "If I can't help myself, how can I help the rest of the congregation?"

I suggest that if these seemingly gentle, caregiving images are *the* central images of ministry, we are hooked into a hierarchical and isolating way of thinking that puts one person above another, helper to helpee. In a discussion of ministerial metaphors, a layman spoke up when we talked about the image of "shepherd" saying, "I don't like that. If the minister is the shepherd, then I am a sheep!"

He grasped quickly that this put him in a inferior position. To the extent that clergy, spouses and laity accept these metaphors, they reinforce the tendency to put clergy on pedestals.

From a pedestal, it is very hard to allow one's humanity to show, and to seek support for oneself when needed it is needed.

Furthermore, acceptance of these metaphors make for high stress in ministry. Roy Oswald puts it this way:

> If our mission is to serve people, we view everyone in need as the call of God to which we must respond. Not to respond is to be guilty of rejecting God's demand on us. Anyone in need in my parish, or even outside my parish, was God's call to me to serve. When I didn't or couldn't, I failed to do what God expected of me. This view of the call of God led me into an adversary relationship with my people. Every time they needed something of me, it was God calling me. But their needs were insatiable. In my exhaustion I saw my people as my enemy. They were destroying my marriage with their demands, they were wreaking havoc with my body, my prayer life, my significant relationships. Yet to say "no" to their demands resulted in guilt for having failed God.
>
> Instead, I need to view as first and foremost God's call to be liberated and whole. I need to apply God's grace to myself first, and to respond by living a joyful, serene life in the midst of my people. My mission would not only be to preach the liberating word of Grace to my people, but also to model a way for them to live by that grace. Grace is God's response to our human condition. Part of what it means to be human is to fail, to experience fatigue, to be finite, to need relationships and support. When I attempt, out of my own human resources, to meet the sea of human need around me, I attempt to be both omnipotent and omnipresent. These are more characteristic of God than humans. When I act this way, I sin like Adam and Eve in their temptation to be like God (1982, pp. 39-40).

If the metaphors of helper, caregiver, shepherd lead us toward an omnipotent, omnipresent, unsupported style of ministry, what other choices do we have? I discovered that there are other commonly held ministry metaphors as well: "companion," "enabler," "spiritual friend." Some individuals describe this as being a person "alongside" others on the spiritual journey, sometimes leading and sometimes being led. They talk about a relationship where there is mutuality. They affirm and accept their special leadership function in the church and their special gifts, but there is a different flavor in how they see themselves in relationship to parishioners. They are both teacher *and* learner; they are both helper *and* receiver of help; they are prophet, pastor, priest, and also enable others in their congregations to claim these roles for themselves in their ministries. Persons who see ministry in these images find it easier to be in touch with their own needs and seek support.

What I have described sounds like two distinct groups, one emphasizing a more hierarchical relationship to parishioners and one emphasizing mutuality on the journey. Though there may be some truth to this division, it is too neatly categorized. I propose instead, a continuum. We all tend to fit somewhere on that continuum, and just where we place ourselves may differ from time to time. However, *when our dominant metaphor is more hierarchical (meaning we minister to the people) rather than a metaphor of partnership and mutuality, (meaning we minister with the people) our ability to seek support and be open to receiving it will suffer.*

One of the key pressures that shapes our metaphors is *how ministry is viewed by our congregations and communities.* Here, we are often dealing with more powerful images than that of "helper." We would be naive if we did not take seriously the images that are projected on the clergy by people in their parishes. If people see the minister, at either conscious or unconscious levels, as "resident holy man/woman," or the "numinous personality," there will be great resistance to seeing the clergyperson as fellow-seeker, sinner, human being, friend and companion. Even if clergypersons wish to work with metaphors of mutuality which embrace the concept of ministry by the whole people of God, they are still confronted by other people's images of ministry and their resistance to change them. It is usually easier and more secure for clergy and their spouses to accept and try to live out the images that people impose on them than to try to change them. John C. Harris says there is

> ... a widespread and deeply felt wish to enshrine pastors as heroes. Pastors often share this wish as well. It is rooted in our fear of creatureliness, of vulnerability. The effect of this wish is to force clergy to be unreal with themselves and their parishes. It makes it tough for ministers to express their own needs, expose vulnerability, be reasonably spontaneous about feelings, moods and judgments. The pastor often ends up acting a role (p. 55).
> ... Furthermore, we are reluctant to take risks with whatever gives us bread and belonging. And if we look to the same source for our recognition and fulfillment as well, our reluctance to risk, to be vulnerable, is even greater (p. 94).

Clyde Reid (1974) takes this a step further. He says that the "holy man" myth must die, and he describes the myth this way:

God has set aside a special group of people who are not ordinary humans, but who have godlike qualities of moral perfection, freedom from temptation and sinfulness and who are possessed with a special wisdom. These men (mostly men of course) can answer all questions and solve all problems. They speak for God, know God intimately, and can make things right for us with God. Those of us within the clergy, though well aware that the myth is a lie, still enjoy its special privileges enough that we don't want to spoil the show. (p. 42) Furthermore, if clergy believe this myth then their dark side, lulled to sleep by their smugness about being "holy," erupts in some unguarded moment (p. 44).

The movie *Cool Hand Luke* presented a provocative picture of what happens when a person is romanticized or deified. Luke, the lead character, arrives as a new prisoner on a prison farm. He remains a bit aloof and separate from the other prisoners and performs a few feats that are impressive and dramatic. The prisoners, perhaps because of their own need for a hero, build a mystique of invincibility around him. He gains a heroic aura, which he encourages because of the power it gives to him. He does all sorts of things to enhance his reputation. Finally, the image he has built gets too heavy to carry, and he breaks under it, exploding with the frustration caused by his fellow prisoners expecting him to be something he is not. The prisoners, in anger and disbelief, don't want to accept that he is other than their hero. What a provocative discussion this movie might provide for a group of clergy and laity! I have met few clergy (and spouses) who have not felt the weight of the clergy image. Perhaps *Cool Hand Luke* can remind us how seductive the mystique of a role can be, and how great the danger in fostering it. Maybe some of us intuitively know this, and that is why pedestals make us so uncomfortable. Maybe that is also why, when we find ourselves put on these pedestals, we resist disillusioning the people who have put us there, fearing that we will lose our effectiveness and become recipients of their anger. Yet, unless we constantly set some limits on what we are able to do, and support the concept of mutual ministry, we will be feeding people's illusions.

What happens when clergy and spouses risk sharing vulnerability and resist pedestals intentionally? Do they lose their credibility as leaders and ministers? The stories I heard would suggest not, provided that they share their humanness in an appropriate way. For instance, it would not be appropriate to use the pulpit to do one's own therapy. It would, however, be appropriate to share one's own woundedness as a way of pointing to the brokenness, forgiveness and grace that is central to our faith. Let me use direct quotes to illustrate what some clergy have discovered, and how one lay person responded to a clergyperson who did share.

> Sharing myself opens up my ministry. Because of some sharing I did, a woman recently came to me with a problem that had been on her heart for 33 years. I think clergy will have more love and respect if they are human. (A clergywoman)

> Since I told others about my illness, people are more willing to share with me than when it seemed like I had it all together. It's easier for them to tell me about _their_ vulnerability. (A clergyman)

> When I exposed my vulnerability, it facilitated my ministry rather than got in the way. The feedback I got was that early in my ministry I was so cool and aloof that people didn't feel they could get close to me. When I shared, it gave other people permission to share with me. (A clergyman)

> When my minister lets us know about some of his struggles with faith and living the Christian life, I move light-years ahead on my journey. (A lay person)

We need to risk being real, not only for the sake of ourselves, but for the sake of others. Henry Nouwen, in his well-known book, _The Wounded Healer_ (1972), reminds us that our wounds are one of the greatest openings for ministry. We need to discover how to share these in ways that will make them a source of healing to others. Robert Raines calls our wounds "the visa into the country of another person's deep being" (Leavitt, 1982, p. 17). It is only in our sharing that we give permission for other people to open up their woundedness to the possibility of healing.

At the heart of this tension between congregations and clergy is a theological issue: what are clergy called to be in the community of faith? An even more basic question is, what is the church community called to be? Without an answer to these two questions, it is impossible to deal with what our metaphors for ministry should be.

We can look at the Church in many ways, but surely a central concept is that of the body of Christ. Furthermore, this community is based on the new covenant given to us by God through Christ. Throughout the Bible, God is seen as a covenanting God. Walter Brueggemann, an Old Testament scholar, suggests that those in covenant "cannot embrace without being transformed by ones who are embraced" (1980, p. 1095). In both the Old and New Testaments, we see a God who covenants with people who can reject Him/Her,

and often do. We see a God very much involved in the pain and
vulnerability of human life.

> The God of the Covenant is not a self-sufficient God. This God
> makes a move to receive sinners and eats with them (Luke 15:2)
> and thus chooses covenant partners with whom things are very
> much at stake, with whom things are yet to be decided. The Bib-
> lical notion of covenant therefore points to a mutual process
> providing opportunities for transformation of its participants
> (Professional Ethics Group, p. 9).

Therefore, we can say that the purpose of the church is to act as
the broken body of Christ for the transformation of the world and
of each other.

> Within the body, the members are to operate, not for their own
> enjoyment or enhancement, but to the end that the body as a
> whole is built up. Each member has equal investment in the life
> of the body and equal responsibility for its existence. Each
> member is as much a part of the church as anyone else is. The
> church that takes the new covenant of God in Christ seriously is
> the church in which participation and community decision are
> required of each member (Ibid., p. 10).

The clergy are called from the midst of the church community
to provide leadership and to help the church function as the body
of Christ. They have responsibility and accountability to God and
the whole body, as do each of the members. All parts must use
their special gifts for the good of the whole body (Romans 12).

Herein lies the difficulty. How many church members see the
church as a covenanting community or understand their participa-
tion in these terms? Protestants, of course, from the time of Martin
Luther, have emphasized the "priesthood of all believers." In recent
years there has been a resurgence of emphasis on the "ministry of
the laity." "Mutual ministry," a term James Fenhagen uses in his
book by that name, holds a model of ministry that is congruent with
a covenanting community. Yet our churches still flounder in making
these concepts a reality. Religion is still "clericalized" for many
church members. These faithful members see themselves as helping
the "real" ministers (the clergy) with their jobs. They have not
claimed their own ministries or come to see themselves as equals
in worth and accountability before God.

We might be tempted to say that the problem is with the lay
people. If only they understood the church and their own call to
ministry, then they would have no need to put clergy on a pedestal.

No doubt this ideal solution would alleviate much of the problem. People would be involved in a community of mutual transformation and would be busy claiming their *own* ministries rather than projecting their religious needs and expectations on the clergy. Clergy could then bring their gifts and perform special leadership and sacramental functions, and be free of being *the* "symbolic religious person." Ideal, but unreal, we might say. Yet if this is our goal, what might we do to move toward it?

I suggest that we clergy and spouses begin with ourselves. If we risked sharing more of our humanity and resisted the "resident holy man/woman" or "omni-competent" images, it might open the way for congregations to begin to grasp more fully their roles in a "covenanting community." *We need to find ways to transfer the congregation's dependence on clergy to our mutual dependence or interdependence on God.* "The greatest gift a pastor has to give another is not the right answer, but the authenticity of his or her own search." (Fenhagen, 1977, p. 105) As long as the clergyperson is driven internally to try to meet all religious needs, to live up to all expectations, and to pretend that he/she is superhuman, this will block people from claiming their personal relationship with God and claiming their own ministries, and this will continue to make it difficult for clergy to seek support when they need it. The process of transformation in a covenanting community happens only in interdependence. This can only come about if clergy are willing to cast off the superhuman projections. In Henry Nouwen's words, "If the preacher does not want to increase the resistance against the Word, but decrease it, he has to be willing to lay himself down and make his own suffering and his own hope available to others so that they can find their own often difficult way" (1971, p. 40).

Am I suggesting that clergy should never allow people to depend on them, or act out of their need for a representative of God to minister to them? Of course not. Clearly there are times when we all need to be dependent. Based on studies of the Grubb Institute, Bruce Reed maintains that there is a normal oscillation process between external and internal dependence. There are times when we all need a relationship with an outside person which enables us to pause sufficiently to regain a sense of well-being and to reorder our inner world (Reed, 1984, p. 2). And there are times when people need to depend on clergy who represent the numinous until they have reordered their world and again can lay claim to the God within. At these times they may invest respected people with a power greater than they really have. One clergywoman, recognizing this, states that she is willing to play that role for people in special need. When someone is grieving, that is not the time to question their "holy man/woman" projection. The danger is that if we continue to play this role all the time, we keep people dependent on us, rather than pointing them to the God on whom we are mutually dependent. The challenge for clergy is to learn to live with the tension between leadership and the authentic and reflective sharing of their own journeys in a community where they are among equals before God.

We have a supreme model for this kind of ministry in Jesus who consistently claimed no authority for himself. He kept reminding people that he came to do the will of another. Donald Winslow, professor at Episcopal Theological Seminary in Cambridge, Mass., explores the source of real authority for Jesus and us:

> The New Testament word for authority is *exousia*, a word which means, literally, out of (one's) essence or being. To be authoritative, then, might be the equivalent of what we normally refer to as being "authentic," living out of who one really is, being one's true self. As for Jesus, in spite of what others said of him, he was most authoritative, most authentic, when he acknowledged that his true self was transparent to the sources of his selfhood. "Why call me good?" he asked. Or when so often his teaching or healing evoked admiration or even idolatrous praise, he pointed to God, not to himself, as the one to be thanked, the one to be praised. Jesus stepped out of the way so that we could have a relationship with God (1979, p. 3).

Our authority comes from the authenticity of the real relationships we work out with our congregations and with our God, not just from our role.

Clarifying our roles is not an easy issue for any of us, clergy, spouses or congregations. So much of the need for putting people on pedestals, or relishing being there, comes out of deep and unconscious needs. But from my interviews, I am aware of at least four tangible things that some clergy and spouses are doing which seem to clarify the issue of roles and metaphors for themselves and their congregations. I share them as possibilities for us to consider.

1) *We can define our role to ourselves and challenge our metaphors.* This is both a theological and personal issue. We need to define our role in terms of who is head of the church we serve, and where healing and hope ultimately come from. We need to gain clarity about what our personal strengths and weaknesses are and learn to be interdependent with others. If we can't define our roles for ourselves, how can we expect that anyone else will be clear about who we are and what they can expect of us?

2) *We can define and keep redefining our roles to the people in our congregations.* They don't know who we are or what our role is unless we tell them. Neither do they know what to expect of a spouse unless this is clarified. Defining our roles to others helps move us out of pretending that we can be "all things to all people." It also gives non-ordained ministers places to use their gifts. When Bruce Larson came as Senior Minister to the large University Presbyterian Church in Seattle, he told his congregation, "Let me describe myself. I have an extraordinary measure of faith; I believe anything is possible with God. I also have a great gift of hope; I really believe that tomorrow is going to be the dawn of the Christian era. But where I got short-changed is in the area of love. I'm insecure, I'm touchy, I'm critical, I'm fault-finding—help me! I'm not a very good lover at all." (Larsen, 1984, p. 15). He was open about his strengths and weaknesses and asked for help. He gained people's respect and at the same time deflected projections of perfection. A clergy wife I met with told how she was at first overwhelmed by many expectations, but she learned that if she gently, but firmly, kept defining herself to the congregation, they were quite willing to accept and love her. Another clergyman said: "If I define myself and my job, people are usually willing to accept my limitations."

3) *We can risk sharing our humanity with our congregations.* We can begin to see this sharing as essential to our ministry. It is one of the doors to creating a covenantal, transforming community. I know that for people like me, who grew up with the message to "put your best foot forward," and whose first inclination is to cover weakness, this is not easy. But, the alternative is personal isolation, which is in contradiction to that which we teach. If we show only our strengths and hide our weaknesses, we encourage others to do likewise, and our churches become museums for the display of successful lives rather than the communities that live by the grace of God.

4) *We can believe in, preach about, and act on our faith that ministry belongs to the whole people of God.* "To push for new interactive forms of partnership between pastors and laity signals a trend toward understanding the church's ministry, not as the ministry of one person, but of a community." (Harris, 1982, p. 49) There are many possibilities for witnessing to the ministry of the whole people. One minister frequently makes a point of acknowledging that there are members of the church who minister to him as much as he ministers to them. Others find ways to identify and affirm the variety of gifts that are being used both

within the church and in the world by its members. All actions that support the belief that clergy are in the church to "equip the saints," not to *be* the saint, helps to undercut the "holy man/woman" myth.

In conclusion, I believe that our ability to live interdependent, supported, authentic lives is intimately connected to how we understand our roles as ministers and spouses of ministers. Our faith and our times are calling us to question and clarify our metaphors for ministry and, if necessary, develop fresh ones. To paraphrase the Rilke quote that was used at the beginning of this chapter, "We must give birth to new images of ministry. These images are the future of ministry waiting to be born."

CHAPTER VI

Underlying Stumbling Blocks to Getting Support: Lack of Self-Esteem and Self-Knowledge

This song was on my first album, but I can sing it better now, so I redid it. The reason I sing it better is that I've been working on me instead of on my singing. You can work on your singing a lot, but after a while you have got to work on where the music comes from. (Song writer Mason Williams)

You shall love the Lord your God with all your heart, with all your soul, with all your mind. You shall love your neighbor as *yourself*. (Matthew 22:37 & 39)

We need to. . .enter first of all into the center of our existence and become familiar with the complexities of our inner lives. As soon as we feel at home in our own house, discover the dark corners as well as the light spots, the closed doors as well as the drafty rooms, our confusion will evaporate, our anxiety will diminish and we will become capable of creative work. (Nouwen, 1972, p. 38)

The crucial factor in what happens both inside people and between people is the picture of worth that each person carries around with him. (Satir, 1972, p. 21)

Sooner or later our solitude will catch up with us and we must find out if it is possible to live with the most difficult companion of all— ourselves. (Palmer, Fall 1985, p. 1)

Hypothesis: Our self-knowledge and sense of worth are key issues in determining whether we are able to get the support we need.

As we look beneath the obvious at what hinders clergy and clergy spouses from finding the support they need, we have considered the cultural and sexual script patterns and the clergy and clergy spouse role. Even more basic than these two potential stumbling blocks are how clergy and their spouses feel about themselves as people, not just how they feel about their role. Obviously, this issue is one that *all* people deal with, but it is helpful to look at self-esteem and self-knowledge from the perspective of why some clergy and spouses get support and some do not. One person who works with clergy commented, "The strong clergy get the support they need, and the weak ones don't." All persons go through difficult times, and when these times come, people who have a solid sense of who they are find it is easier to reach out for the necessary support.

We have been going through a period where the emphasis on personal growth and self-affirmation has topped the best-seller lists and turned into a big business. It speaks of a deep hunger in many people. It also produced what has been called the "me generation." Lest we who call ourselves Christian too easily dismiss this popular emphasis on the self, let us look a little closer, and find what is basic to our best psychological and Christian understandings.

I believe that when Jesus said that one of the great commandments was to love your neighbor *as yourself*, the phrase, "as yourself," was highly significant. Self-love is intimately connected with neighbor-love and even with the love of God. When we lack self-love or self-esteem, it permeates how we approach much of the rest of life. Low self-esteem can encourage us to foster the pedestal image of clergy. As one clergyperson said: "Some of us need the clergy image because we are insecure. I really have to fight that." Low self-esteem can encourage us to be workaholics, equating worth with our performance. Low self-esteem can encourage unhealthy dependency, or a facade of total self-sufficency, rather than allowing us to mature into interdependent relationships. Low self-esteem can lead us to be so obsessed with pleasing others that we lose a sense of who we are. Lack of self-love can prevent us from taking the time and actions necessary for our own physical, mental and emotional well-being, for we quickly neglect that which we do not value. Low self-esteem cripples our ability to truly love other people. Finally, lack of self-love gets in the way of reaching out for the support we need.

Adler believed that an inferiority complex is the key dynamic behind people's striving for superiority over others. (Ellison, 1983, p. 2) Could this be at the root of the competitiveness that many say they feel at clergy gatherings? I know that when I am in a group of fellow professionals, one of the subtle ways I defend against my insecurity is to share all the things that are going well and hide those things that are not. I present myself as strong and hide my vulnerability. To the extent that others play this same game, the results are a competitive interchange rather than real sharing.

Karen Horney emphasized that we need to value ourselves in order to value others. If we put ourselves down, we are likely to encourage others to put us down as well (Ellison, 1983, p. 2). Clergy and spouses who discount their own needs encourage others to do the same. Also, to the extent that we are insecure and do not value ourselves, the tendency will be to keep people dependent on us rather than be enablers of their claiming their own strength.

Learning to know and affirm oneself is especially important for clergy. We live and work in a society where prestige and money are considered to be sources of self-esteem. Obviously, clergy are not going to be able to bolster their self-esteem by what they earn. The clergy role may still be an honored one, but, as we indicated earlier, clergy are no longer automatically given the same status in community and congregation that they once were. Questions currently being raised about the meaning of ordination and the reclaiming of the ministry of the laity may be shaking some of the traditional sources of self-esteem. The less clergy can depend on the externals for self-esteem, the more imperative it is that they strengthen the internal ones.

Learning to know and affirm oneself is equally important for clergy spouses. The role of clergy spouse has often encouraged wives to feel like mere appendages to their husbands, rather than unique individuals with God- given gifts to be used. One clergy wife said, "I used to see myself as riding in a side-car of a motorcycle that my husband was driving. I had no control over the direction we were going. I was just along for the ride. After many years of change and a new career, I now see myself riding my own motorcycle, sometimes going in my own crazy directions and sometimes going in the same direction as my husband." The basic issue isn't whether a wife has her own career, or is spending her time sharing in the ministry as a volunteer. The issue is how she *feels* about it, and whether she has made a *choice* based on her gifts. The issue is whether she can affirm her worth in the midst of her choice. Where male spouses of clergy are concerned, their own sense of self-worth is basic to how they will react to their wives being in the clergy role. My limited data in the area of male spouses suggests there is probably less chance that they will feel like they are riding in a side car and more chance that they will feel they have been relegated to the backseat because of the time-demands on their wives. This too is a self-worth issue, and must be dealt with for their own sakes and the sake of their marriages.

Self-love, self-esteem or self-affirmation is obviously not to be equated with the popular "I AM NUMBER ONE" mentality. People with genuine self-esteem do not need to be "number one" or always right. What I am urging is a fundamental sense that we are persons of worth, with unique gifts that we are called to use. This is affirmed by popular psychology which states that "I'm ok and you're ok." However, when we ask, how do we *know* that we are ok, there is silence! The Christian has a much more solid undergirding for self-love. We have a theology that affirms that we are created in the image of God and that this creation was good (Genesis 1:26-28). We have a faith that witnesses to the belief that "we love because God first loved us." This redemptive act of unconditional love forms the foundation of Christian self-love. If God values us, then we can value ourselves.

Often that which we profess to believe does not find its way into our innermost being. Some of us have a heritage that has bred into us a sense of our unique worth and the worth of others, enabling us to live with a predisposition toward security and trust, and allowing us to use our gifts and share our vulnerablity. However, the majority of us tend to bring to our living a lot of insecurity, self-doubt, uncertainty about the gifts we have, and a lack of self-love. If we are to be liberated from this low self-esteem, or at least learn to live creatively with it, we have to work intentionally at it.

There are at least three intentional ways that clergy and their spouses can add to their self-knowledge and self-esteem.

1) *One way is through psychotherapy.* Numerous persons I spoke with testified to the value of this experience in their lives. Often this was more of an educational growth experience than a medical necessity. Working with a trained professional in a counseling or therapeutic setting may help individuals learn to affirm themselves, to face and deal with difficult experiences and transitions in more creative ways, and to develop more open relationships. It also helps them to deal with unfinished business from their past that is complicating their present living.

2) *Another way is the opening up of their spiritual journeys.* This could mean working with a spiritual director, a "spiritual friend," or a spiritual growth group. The process may be aided by journal-writing, work with dreams, prayer and meditation practice, and "the healing of memories," or whatever keeps us open to the transforming power of God in our lives. It is this power that affirms and undergirds our sense of worth.

3) *Finally, a number of clergy and a few spouses spoke about the value of a support group of colleagues or friends.* Such groups can provide "safe places" to be oneself, to grow with those who share common concerns, to learn to trust showing

vulnerability, to be lovingly confronted when needed, and to be affirmed in weakness and in strength.

These kinds of supports for growth need to be seen as integral parts of ministry, not as extras for those who can't cope! There are many opportunities to develop better skills in ministry (the "how-to" opportunities such as increasing membership, preaching better, stewardship, etc.). These are important because they not only improve the job that clergy do, but they aid self-confidence. However, as Mason Williams said, "*sometimes we have to work on where the music comes from.*" Clergy and their spouses need adequate opportunities and encouragement to work on where the music comes from, so that they may grow in self-knowledge and self-worth.

Conclusion

In these last three chapters we have considered three underlying factors that make it difficult for many clergy and spouses to get the support they need: 1) cultural and sexual script patterns; 2) metaphors for ministry, or the way we view the clergy role; and 3) lack of self-knowledge or self-esteem. There are no "easy fixes" for any of these. Yet it seems essential that clergy and their spouses find ways to deal with them for their own well-being and for the sake of the church. Ministry has to do with supporting and enabling people to become the liberated and whole people that God intends them to be. How can we invite and support others on this journey if we have not been willing to go on the inner journey ourselves, dealing with some of the complexities of our own lives? It is through the sharing of our own personal and spiritual growth toward wholeness that we enable others on their journeys. This lifelong journey entails learning and relearning *who and whose we are*. All of us need to find the resources that keep calling us back to this journey and support us on the way.

CHAPTER VII

Resources for Support: What Works and What Doesn't!

In spite of the underlying barriers to gaining support, most clergy and their spouses do have some support. What supports are working well for them and what aren't? The purpose of this chapter is to present some of the findings that emerged from the interviews and questionnaires regarding these supports.

First, some general observations:

1) It is clear that no one way of getting support is right for everyone. What is effective for one person may not be for another.

2) It was borne out in the interviews and by the data from the questionnaire that individuals will choose different kinds of people for support depending on the nature of the issue and the kind of support needed. Most of us need a varied support network.

3) External circumstances influence where people find support. Two of the most significant external circumstances that shape our options are marital status and geographical location. The single person usually does not have the built-in support that a spouse provides. Professional and collegial support are less readily available to those living in more isolated areas.

4) Those persons who have the best support systems have them because they value supportive relationships enough to give them some priority, and are willing and able to take some initiative. In many cases, the valuing of supportive relationships came only after breaking free from some of the personally limiting issues that were described earlier (such as cultural and sexual scripts and low self-esteem). In some cases, people indicated that they found their supportive relationships almost by chance. For example two persons meet at a clergy gathering, a rapport is experienced, a friendship is formed and a support system is

enlarged. Yet, even in these circumstances, it took initiative and some intentionality for the relationship to develop. Trusted relationships take time and commitment.

Beyond these general observations, here are some learnings regarding the availability and effectiveness of existing support systems:

A. Support from Spouses

Spouses (male and female) are the main source of support for most clergy. As one clergyman said, "It's wonderful to know that I can go home to a safe place and, at my own speed, let it all come out." Male clergy rely even more heavily on their spouses as their *sole* support than female clergy do on their husbands. Single clergy, not having this "spouse support" option, have to work harder at developing a primary source of support.

Obviously, "spouse support" is only as good as the marriage relationship itself. Many clergy marriages are under enormous pressure from lack of time and many other stresses. This underlines the need to find ways to nurture marriages, such as marriage enrichment groups, opportunities for increasing listening and communication skills, and affordable opportunities to get away as a couple.

Generally, support for female spouses is less available than for either male or female clergy. Though many wives spoke of their husbands as a major source of support, a significant number of wives played the role of being the principal "absorber" of their husbands' problems, and have fewer opportunities to share their own problems with husbands or others. A woman who used to be a spouse of a clergyman said: "When I was a clergy spouse, I would take in all his problems, but I had no one to talk to. I guess I figured that I wasn't worth taking my problems to anybody, and I didn't know whom to go to."

Spouse support, though obviously important, has some limitations. When the problem causing pain is the marriage itself, then support needs to come from outside. Also the marriage support system tends to break down when both persons are in pain or under serious stress at the same time. Another problem in relying too heavily on "spouse support" as the *only* support is that the husband or wife is often so emotionally involved that he/she can not provide the necessary objectivity.

The importance of the marriage relationship cannot be overestimated, but there is a real danger in relying on it too completely. There need to be additional good sources of support for both partners individually. Several clergy and spouses indicated that when they were providing each other's sole support, it was a very heavy burden. Expressing need for additional support, one clergyman said, "It would be nice to have a deep, sharing relationship with someone else besides my wife. I don't want my wife carrying the whole load. It would be enriching to our marriage relationship if I had other people to share with in addition to my wife."

B. Support from Parishioners

Robert Kemper suggests that the preferred pastoral decorum for friendships with parishioners would seem to be "open to all and entangling alliances with none". (1985, p. 127) Many clergy and spouses sense that this is true. There continues to be considerable anxiety around having close friends in the parish. Clergy and their spouses are aware that they have to filter what they say to parishioners. Several clergy observed that being open about their vulnerability *after* a crisis often seems to enhance relationships, but having parishioners deeply involved in the midst of some kinds of crises is destructive of leadership.

However, I found that some clergy and their spouses do form very supportive relationships within their parishes. This seems easier to do in larger parishes and in city areas than in small towns and small churches. It also seems that the most frequent in-depth sharing in these relationships is around parish concerns and common interests, rather than about deeply personal issues. In spite of these limitations, let's not underestimate this important area of support. The Mills and Koval study (1971) indicates that almost two-thirds of clergy stress comes from job-related issues. In my study, over half of the clergy polled indicated that they had experienced "major conflict with parishioners or staff" and that in the midst of this issue the majority turned to other parishioners for support. Numerous clergy and spouses spoke about having a few very trusted friends in the parish.

There were only a few among the 47 persons I interviewed who believed that they could not have *any* friendships within the parish. Yet almost all agreed that there were handicaps and limits on these friendships. Supportive relationships within the parish are important, but they usually do not provide the freedom and depth of relationships that are outside the parish.

C. Support from Denominational Leadership

When clergy and spouses were asked if there were adequate resources in our denominational structures to provide the support
they need for personal issues (Appendix III), about 50% responded
that there were not adequate resources. About 25% of the respondents were uncertain whether or not there were resources at all.
What is this telling us?

In every UCC Conference, and in most other mainline denominations, there are one or more persons who have as part of their
job being "minister to the ministers." This is based on the belief
that pastors need pastors. For some (slightly less than half of the
clergy interviewed), this relationship with Conference staff proved
to be very helpful during times of personal need. In Appendix IV,
you will note that the primary issue that is taken to Conference staff
has to do with church-related problems such as a major conflict
with parishioners or staff. Both the questionnaire and my interviews
indicate that clergy share personal issues with denominational personnel to a considerably lesser degree than they share professional
or church related issues.

In any case, if these "ministers to the ministers" are so helpful,
why are they not used more often by clergy?

1) *Over half of the clergy interviewed indicated that they would
not share their vulnerability with persons who had anything to
do with placement.* "It might color my job opportunities," said
one person. "One day he might need to write a reference for
me, so I wouldn't feel comfortable sharing personal things with
him," said another. "They (Conference personnel) are in an ov-
erseer role."

2) *Individuals who do not have a trusting relationship with an
Area or Conference Minister have trouble talking with them
about personal issues.* "I don't bare my soul until I trust people."
Trusting relationships are built on contact and empathy, and frequently there have not been opportunities to achieve that with
denominational leaders. As one person said, "I haven't had even
a call from a Conference person in three years." Where clergy
have been able to build a trusting relationship because of
chance circumstances or because the Area Minister found ways
to reach out and develop relationships, there is much more
readiness to turn to this source of support.

3) *Conference Ministers and Area Ministers aren't always seen as
accessible.* In some cases this meant that they were not the kind

of people that one would turn to for pastoring or counseling, and that they too often "came with their own agenda." But for many more persons, it was a simple recognition that these Conference staff are already overburdened. This was especially true in Conferences such as Massachusetts, where these Conference leaders have a responsibility for a large number of churches and clergy as well as programs. In small Conferences such as Rhode Island, a much more personal relationship seems possible. In geographically spread-out conferences like Nebraska, Iowa and California, lack of accessibility is partially due to distance.

4) *Conference persons are perceived as being concerned primarily with "the job," and are not expected to be available for personal issues.* They were sometimes seen as persons with a primary responsibility to the churches, rather than to the clergy. Obviously, the needs of the clergy and the needs of the churches are sometimes in conflict.

With one exception, the clergy spouses I interviewed perceived that the Conference "minister to the ministers" was not available to them. The results of the questionnaire confirm that few spouses turn to Conference Ministers (Appendix V). Three clergy wives spoke with particularly strong feelings about episodes where Area or Conference Ministers came to see their husbands in the midst of a family crisis, but showed little concern that they, the wives, were also in pain. Studies of clergy divorce also indicate that when a divorce takes place, the focus of the denominational people tends to be on the clergy and not the spouse. Some Conference Ministers acknowledged that it is hard to know how to minister to clergy spouses. It is often said that the pastor has no pastor; it is even more true that spouses have "no pastors," because they are married to a pastor, and because they feel there are few denominational resources open to them.

Whether these feelings about denominational leaders are justified or not, my interviews and the questionnaires suggest that this is a significant support issue for a number of clergy and spouses.

Some Conferences are finding ways to address some of these issues. The Pennsylvania UCC Conferences, in conjunction with several other denominations, provide three counselors for clergy families. Associated with the Bethany Counseling Center, they provide marriage and family counseling, family life education, consultation to the pastors and liaison with the Conference staff. Of particular importance is the fact that though these counselors are affiliated with the UCC Conference, they have no role in placement and maintain confidentiality about their clients. Counseling fees run from $1 to $35 so that limited finances do not prevent any clergy family from getting assistance. This makes counseling more accessible than in many other Conferences, and does not entail clergy or spouses having to ask leaders in the denominational structure for counseling funds.

The Connecticut Conference of the UCC has recently instituted a "Clergy Wellbeing Program." This is an employee assistance program aimed at providing education, assessment, referral and support without any direct connection to Conference personnel. The initial thrust is aimed at chemical dependence, but the aim is to expand it to cover the full range of problem areas. It is too soon to know how effective this will be.

Counseling arrangements such as these still do not address the issue of who does the pastoring which is needed *before* issues reach crisis proportions. The Iowa Conference staff seeks to address this need by regular contact with pastors. This includes a phone call every sixty days to all pastors, and a personal visit for those going through some particular crisis. The written reponses that I received from Iowa clergy generally indicate that they feel supported by the Conference staff. How much of this positive feeling is due to the regular contacts, and how much to the other Conference offerings is impossible to ascertain from my data. Still many of the Iowa clergy indicated that it would be helpful to have a "minister to ministers" who was not associated with placement. Generally the Conference personnel I interviewed did not think that being involved in placement was a conflict of interest for them when "ministering to the ministers." But many local clergy *do* see this to be a serious issue.

Denominational support comes through programs as well as individual pastoral contacts. It is helpful, for example, to have workshops aimed at skill-development and specific stages of ministry such as "Clergy in Transition" (offered in Connecticut) or "Pre-retirement Conferences" (offered in Massachusetts) or "Clergy and Crisis" workshops (in Iowa).

A number of clergy and their wives spoke of special needs for support during the early years of ministry. This support might come from older clergy and spouses "who had already been there." The support might come from gathering together fellow clergy and spouses who are also new to the parish. A few new clergy reached out and gained support from a retired minister in their congregation or from a colleague, but more often they did not know where to turn. Initiative from the denomination would have been very valuable at this point.

Opportunities for spouses differ widely from Conference to Conference. In many parts of the country clergy spouses feel that there is little offered that supports them. This troubles some, but is of little concern to others. Several spoke of feeling unacknowledged, and wished they would at least be invited to the orientation session which is held for new ministers. Some Conferences have tried a few ways of addressing this issue. For example, Northern California and Nebraska have successful annual retreats for spouses; Massachusetts and Rhode Island offer Marriage Enrichment for Clergy Couples; Nebraska offers Covenant Support Groups for couples.

I heard special appreciation for opportunities that were aimed at supporting clergy and their spouses as *people*, not just as professionals. The Shalom Retreats for clergy and spouses that were held in Massachusetts about 15 years ago were referred to a number of times. These Shalom Retreats began to address some of the issues that were described in the chapters dealing with the hidden blocks to getting support. Furthermore, these Shalom Retreats provided some follow-up support in the form of "house churches" that were very meaningful to a significant number of persons. The on-going groups were a crucial ingredient of this support experience.

Another key support that some Conferences make available to clergy (and sometimes to their spouses) is funding for counseling or career-development. Such services are often beyond the financial reach of clergy and spouses. Though many clergy health plans pay 50% of counseling fees, this is not enough when the hourly rate for counseling is between $60 and $120. Again, there is some reluctance to ask for this kind of help through denominational structures and this, in turn, is a deterrent to getting support before things reach a crisis point.

Finally, I discovered that many clergy and spouses are not familiar with the resources that *are* available to them. In Massachusetts, for example, some were surprised to learn that there were funds available for counseling and career development.

D. Support from Colleagues

Many clergy expressed the belief that "clergy aren't very good at ministering to each other," and that many clergy groups are only superficially supportive. The most frequent reasons given for this were:

1) Competitiveness and unwillingness to share vulnerability with colleagues;

2) Isolated work situations that often keep one unaware of another's need;

3) "We all have enough to do taking care of our own parishes." "We have to support people all the time. I can't handle any more";

4) "Seeing a colleague's pain brings it too close to home. It could happen to me";

5) "I'm much more concerned that a colleague will judge the way I try to minister, therefore I often shy away." "I'm afraid I'll look like a fool";

6) "I don't trust fellow clergy, especially in the area of confidentiality";

7) "I often assume that someone else is ministering to a fellow minister and they don't need me";

8) Clergy are afraid that a fellow clergy person will be playing a role. "I need to know if you are in a role or really care, before I share."

Some of the above reasons are given by female clergy as well as male clergy. However, female clergy seem to support each other better than males do. They are more likely to develop support groups and networks, though sometimes these fall by the wayside the longer they are in the ministry and the demands of the job crowd out their personal need for support. Several female clergy said they steered away from offical groups of clergywomen because they tended to end up as gripe sessions about the difficulties of being a woman in ministry. They did not want to be part of groups where people were playing the "victim role," though at the same time recognizing that they needed support from colleagues.

For all clergy, the large, official clergy gatherings seemed to provide only superficial support. Such gatherings have value, but they do not meet the support need for deeply personal issues. They are important for sharing and support at one level, and they provide opportunities to develop relationships that might become more supportive relationships.

Clergy spouses, for the most part, have little meaningful contact with other clergy spouses. In a few localities there are interdenominational clergy wives' groups which meet and talk about common issues. Several clergy wives indicate that they cherish the support from a fellow clergy wife with whom they had developed a friendship during seminary or at a clergy wives' retreat. New clergy wives

wish for more opportunities to share with other wives who are
going through similar situations.

There is another very important side to this story. For some
clergy, friendships and peer support groups are some of the most
significant support they have, and they wouldn't be without them. A
number of ministers meet with one or two colleagues on a regular
basis, even traveling considerable distances to continue this relationship when one person has moved away. As one clergyman said:
"When something goes wrong or the pressure begins to build up, I
just think to myself, it's only five more days until I see Joe, and I
can spill it all. He'll listen, understand, and help me get some perspective."

A number of clergy are part of peer support groups which were
formed because someone took the initiative and asked fellow clergy
if they would like to be part of a group. Occasionally, groups form
around a counselor with whom they contract for supervision of
counseling cases. These groups help the members deal with personal issues as well as provide supervision for their counseling.
One group formed for the purpose of Bible study and to support
each other in preaching and at the same time worked on their life
issues in relationship to the Scripture. Several years ago, the New
Hampshire Conference of the UCC initiated a support group for
clergy couples (in which both are ordained). It was described as a
"life saver" by at least one couple. One Area Minister has a regular
book study group that meets with him. Besides discussing a book,
they talk about personal issues.

There are some common characteristics that enable peer support groups to work. Roy Oswald has done a great deal of work
with clergy groups and he feels that groups work only if they have a
competent leader from outside the group. Though good leadership
can help a group move more quickly beyond the superficial level, I
found that some peer support groups seemed to be working well
without a designated leader. The important ingredients which seem
to determine success are:

1) Common interest or relationships carried over from another
context;

2) Small size of 4-6 persons;

3) One or two persons willing to risk openness and vulnerability; (it is especially helpful if there is a person who is perceived
as being "strong and competent" and who is willing to be vulnerable)

4) Commitment to regular attendance;

5) Ground rules about confidentiality and group process;

6) Regular meetings over a long enough time that trusting relationships are built.

There are those who feel that ecumenical peer support groups are easier and less competitive, but two of the good existing groups I encountered were composed of members of the same denomination.

Some of the testimonies as to what these peer support groups have meant to clergy are quite dramatic.

"I was very depressed, to the point of being suicidal and not being able to act on my own behalf. My clergy group recognized how depressed I really was. They confronted me and got me into therapy and supported me through it."

Other clergy speak of peer groups as providing less dramatic but equally important ongoing support, sustenance, perspective and growth.

The central value of a support group seems to be having a place where one can be honest, accepted, affirmed and supported in growing and in dealing with whatever is going on in one's life. The importance of a group of colleagues is that they talk the same language, hold many of the same values and bring perspective on ministry issues. Clergy need understanding colleagues who can help them be aware of how their role can even destroy the awareness of their need for support. Peer support groups seem to be one of the major defenses against this.

Other opportunities for peer support include: multiple staffs that have developed caring relationships; being part-time on the staff of a counseling center and meeting regularly with the staff. Resource materials can facilitate groups. One clergy couples support group has as its focus, *Clergy Stress, A Survival Kit for Church Professionals* (Oswald, 1982). One couple said that using materials such as the "Survival Kit" and answering the questions that were asked helped them to be more honest and open in the group.

In short, *some* clergy and their spouses are finding significant ways to support and be supported by colleagues. However, many do not have the colleague support they need and want. Finding the ways to enable more colleague support is one of the most challenging areas to be addressed.

E. Support from Friends and Family

"There is no time to develop friendships outside of the parish." This has a familiar ring for many clergy couples. However, some don't settle for this. For my husband and me, some long-time friendships that date back to college years and close friendships with one or two nearby clergy couples have been important. Some clergy couples deliberately seek out persons who have nothing to do with their church. One couple looks for Jewish and Catholic friends, knowing that these persons are not likely to become parishioners at a later date. They find more freedom to "let down their hair" and get away from the job with non-church friends.

Family seems to be a key support for clergy spouses. A comparatively large number clergy wives indicated that "extended family" is a major support for them. Clergy wives speak of grown children, sisters, brothers and parents continuing to be a support. Some of them talked about the difficulty of living at a distance from family. My sense is that family support becomes even more important when other support systems are sparse, as in the case of clergy wives.

Spouses who have a career or job outside the home often find their work relationships to be a source of friendship and support. Employment seems to be a helpful channel for making friends who are not associated with the church.

F. Support from Professional Counseling

Counseling has been a major source of growth and help for many clergy and spouses. It has been a way to address the complexities of one's life. Even when the issues are not completely resolved, counseling can greatly increase emotional energy and often results in more effective ministering. Frequently, it has taken a crisis to initiate counseling. According to the responses (Appendix IV), the main issues that clergy seek counseling for are marital and sexual problems and depression. The spouses who responded to the questionnaire go to counselors less frequently than male or female clergy, and their most common issue seems to be depression (Appendix V). For reasons described in the chapters on underlying blocks to getting support, even in times of crisis there is a great deal of resistance to going for help. The feeling that "we should be able to work it out ourselves" still persists, until things reach a desperation point. Yet those who have discovered the value of counseling with a therapist or pastoral counselor know that it has benefits that extend beyond crisis intervention. Self-knowledge is part of the truth that sets us free.

In addition to the resistance to seeking counseling a major problem is money. There are clergy and spouses who need professional help, but don't have the money, are not aware that there are funds available to help them; or they feel threatened by contacting denominational staff to request these funds. Sometimes clergy and spouses would prefer going to a pastoral counselor, but find that their insurance covers only secular counselors.

G. Support Through Spiritual Renewal

As important as psychological counseling may be, it is not enough. Though in ministry there has always been an emphasis on the spiritual disciplines, there seems now to be an increased hunger for spiritual renewal and a recognition that it is basic to both life and ministry. But along with this hunger there is also a deep-seated suspicion of some kinds of piety. As Tilden Edwards said: "We are surrounded by much American spirituality that strikes us as egotistical, hyped, and evasive of personal and social responsibility" (1985, p. 6). In many clergy and some spouses there is a kind of restlessness and yearning for finding new and meaningful ways to nurture their spiritual life, not as an escape from social responsibility but as a foundation for it. Some of them sense that "burn-out" is often due to lack of meaning or lack of spiritual grounding rather than to over-work.

The biggest frustration for many clergy is that the time needed for spiritual growth is often crowded out by the demands of the job. When this happens, it becomes increasingly hard to provide steady and solid spiritual leadership for their congregations. Clergy cannot provide spiritual nurture for others if their own well is dry. It is an awesome enough challenge to provide ongoing spiritual nurture to a congregation in the midst of the unsteady rhythms that we all know to be part of the normal spiritual life.

How are clergy and clergy spouses seeking to nurture their spiritual growth? Some clergy find that the reading of Scripture and other resources in preparation for preaching feeds their spirits. During the week they may seek to hold in their minds and hearts the Scripture they are working with, letting it interact with their daily lives. Others find that this isn't sufficient, because it is too oriented toward producing something for the nurture of others. Some clergy and spouses develop a practice that is designed for their own

special needs and personalities. For example, it may be a regular
early morning walk that includes prayer and meditation. Journal
writing, working with dreams, yoga, running, gardening, a regular
meditation practice, fasting, attending retreats or being part of a
prayer group which helps nurture spiritual growth within a community setting, taking time for music and the arts, outreach to those in
need, and prayer are all ways that are meaningful.

Clergy and spouses often do not have someone with whom to
share their spiritual journeys. Clergy spouses in particular feel they
have no one to talk with about this (Appendices V, VIII). It is also
interesting to note that clergy talk with their spouses about their
spiritual needs less than any other issue (Appendix IV). Having no
one to talk with can be especially lonely and isolating for clergy
during dry or doubting times, during which one's congregation is
continuing to expect its pastor to be a steady, faith-filled person.
Not being able to share the valleys as well as the peaks contributes
to depression and spiritual dryness. Some clergy are able to be
open about this with their congregations, and find that this en-
hances their parishioners' spiritual growth and their ability to minister to their minister.

A number of people are finding that there is tremendous value
in having a spiritual director or "soul friend." This may be a person
who is trained in the art of spiritual direction, or a colleague with
whom there is mutual sharing. A spiritual director or a soul friend
is a person with whom one meets regularly, and who helps by listening for the signs of the Spirit moving in us. It is someone who
cares for the unique unfolding of the image of God in us and who
will be with us in the wilderness as well as in the faith-filled times.
Many of us find that we put our spiritual growth on hold when life
gets too busy. A regular time with a spiritual friend, a specific disci-
pline, or a group focused on spiritual growth are several ways to
keep this part of us alive and growing.

There is evidence to suggest that the ways in which our individual spiritual lives are nurtured best are often determined by our
personality type (Gilbert, 1984/85, p. 4-15). For example, those persons who are "introverts," according to the Myers-Briggs Type Indi-
cator, often find private prayer and meditation more meaningful
than the "extrovert" and "feeling" types who tend to find corporate
prayer and relationships more significant channels to God. The variety of roads on the spiritual journey needs to be honored in ourselves and others. There is little need for what one clergyperson
called the "great guilt trip at not having a spiritual practice like I see
in other people." However, almost all the persons I talked with

agreed that when they intentionally nurture the spiritual dimension in themselves, their lives and ministries are undergirded and em-powered.

H. Support from Seminary and Continuing Education

President George Peck of Andover Newton Theological School said in an address to students: "The patterns we develop at Andover Newton are the patterns we will carry with us into our ministries." Harbaugh and Rogers (1984, p. 9) confirm that this is an accurate assessment, that there is a remarkable correlation between how students dealt with stress in seminary and and how they dealt with it in the parish. What are the patterns that are developed in seminary? Are the cultural and sexual patterns of independence and self-suffi-cency encouraged or discouraged? Is there encouragement for and modeling of collegial ministry? Is there support for the develop-ment of mind, body and spirit in the preparation of ministers? Are serious questions raised to help students to consider how they will get the support they will need to prevent burn-out in the ministry? Is anyone challenging students to examine their metaphors for min-istry and the ramifications these might have for how they carry out their ministries? Are seminaries helping their future ministers to en-able the ministry of the laity without feeling undermined in their own sense of ministerial self-worth and calling? Is anyone address-ing the stresses on clergy marriages? The questions are endless. Each one of these questions has a human and a theological dimen-sion to it, each one has serious implications for clergy and their spouses finding the support they need.

The issue of seminary training is so basic to the question of clergy support that I want to comment on some of what I learned from my conversations with clergy and seminary students, profes-sors and administrators. Seminaries appear to do a fine job academ-ically, but usually pay scant attention to the body and soul. Also they often fail to provide the necessary training for the realities of parish ministry. This is confirmed by Charles Fielding's 1966 study for the American Association of Theological Schools. "Ministry today is gen-erally discontinuous with the preparation provided for it." He rec-ommends that professional education be understood as "the acquisition of knowledge, the development of professional skill, personal human growth and deepening Christian commitment" (As quoted in Biersdorf, 1985, p. 77). A recent survey of students at An-dover Newton Theological School (Tracy, 1985) concluded that students feel there is little encouragement to take care of one's body or develop the spiritual, personal dimension. Tracy asks the question: "Does not the absence of ongoing personal and group support set forth a pattern for creating 'lone rangers,' ministers who attempt to shoulder alone their personal and professional burdens until they reach a point commonly known as clergy burn-out?" (p. 4)

Some clergy who have been out in the parish for a while indicate that they realize there was not much in seminary that helped them consider the issues that have been raised in this book and that in fact seminaries often reflect the cultural patterns that affect ministry and do not help students challenge these patterns theologically. Seminaries also teach by what is *not* said, or *not* included in the curriculum. Perhaps seminaries cannot be expected to teach holistic life management, but it seems to me that they *do* have some responsibility to model it, discuss it from a personal and theological base, and alert students to the dangers of some of their common metaphors for ministry. (See chapter V.)

If an attitude could be fostered in seminary that education is the *beginning* of training for the ministry, not the end, then some of these questions might be addressed by continuing education beyond the M.Div. degree. Many D. Min. programs continue to emphasize the academic and professional sides of ministry which often bring new breadth of understanding and skills to ministry. Without doubt these are important. What often is missing are the personal, spiritual growth components which are at the heart of support in ministry. One of the unique aspects of the Doctor of Ministry program at the Institute for Advanced Pastoral Studies in Detroit is its emphasis on developing the personal, spiritual undergirding for ministry. The only other continuing education programs that interviewees spoke of as having some personal growth emphasis are those that train for pastoral counseling. These programs helped students become more effective in their ministries by encouraging them to develop an increased awareness of themselves and the human predicament in relation to their theology.

Other short-term opportunities for support through continuing education are offered through denominational structures, seminaries, The Alban Institute and retreat centers like Kirkridge, to mention only a few. Clergy spoke of finding these useful *when* they made time for them, and *if* they could afford them. One study claims that only twenty per cent of all clergy participate in continuing education of any kind during a given year. Obviously, continuing education support works only if clergy use it and it is financially feasible.

I. In Conclusion

John Sanford helps us image the need for support by using the illustration of a sparkling clear lake which stays that way only because it has inlets and outlets. (1982) Streams and deep springs flow into it so that it does not dry up, and the outlets are open so that it does not become stagnant and blocked up. There is a receiving and a giving necessary to keep clarity and foster the life of the lake. So it is with us too.

Some clergy and spouses are satisfied with their resources. They are taking time to nurture supportive relationships with their spouse, parishioners, friends, peers, denominational personnel, counselors, and with themselves and with God. Yet most of these clergy and spouses find that it is a constant battle to make time for the relationships which nurture them. When they neglect these resources too long, they are drained. There are other clergy and spouses who have not found adequate resources (inlets) and to varying degrees therefore are isolated, unsupported and depleted. This becomes accentuated during times when personal problems or crises are most intense. The lack of resources affects both their personal well-being and their ministries.

Are there any new directions or ways of opening up possibilities for clergy and their spouses in order that they might get the support they need? This is a subject we will explore in the next chapter.

CHAPTER VIII

Directions and Possibilities

My aim in this chapter is to collect, present, and summarize some of the specific directions and tangible possibilities for helping clergy and their spouses find the support they need. I will focus first on what individual clergy and spouses can do for themselves; second, on what issues seminaries need to address; and third, what denominational systems can do to provide more support.

A. What Can Individual Clergy and Spouses Do For Themselves?

If clergy and their spouses are going to gain support for coping with stress they will need a *growing sense of who they are, a deepening faith, and a well-developed support system*. Though we cannot force these three things to happen, neither can we sit back passively, waiting for other people to tell us who we are, expecting someone else to take care of providing our support, or anticipating that our spiritual life will deepen with no active initiative or attention from us. Though we cannot *control* all the circumstances of our lives, we can learn to *create* some of our own circumstances. Here are some ways of doing this:

1) *We can take time to nurture the spiritual grounding of our lives.* Ministry is not a vocation that can be lived out over the long haul without this grounding. Nurturing our connectedness with the God we serve is not optional. James Fenhagen claims: "No one becomes a minister. Rather in trust we open ourselves to the Spirit that Jesus Christ can express his ministry through us. Prayer and ministry are indissoluable" (1981, p. 9). It is not enough to remind ourselves that our ultimate support "cometh from the Lord." Jesus

promised us the "living water" (Luke 4:12-15), but we must lower our buckets into the deep. One clergyman told me about a time when he felt fractured and exhausted from trying to be all that his parishioners wanted him to be. He went into the sanctuary and sat down on the floor behind the pulpit where no one would find him. Then he shared with God what he was feeling. And God spoke to him and said, "John, you jerk, be yourself!" Maybe it is only in our relationship with God that we finally come to terms with the fact that God is calling us to be who we are, and that we are free to live by grace.

2) *Since we are called to free ourselves of the stumbling blocks that keep us from being all that God intends,* we can look for ways to explore and deal with our cultural, sexual, personal and clergy script patterns. We need to be willing to ask for help. We need to take the initiative to get spiritual and/or psychological counseling, to talk with denominational staff when needed, and to discover the available resources for continuing on our growth journeys. We need to find individuals or peer groups who can support and challenge us.

If we can live with the belief that we are *becoming* and cast off the seductive belief that we have arrived, then we have the impetus to grow. This in turn will enable those around us to grow. Along with Paul we can say,

> Not that I have already obtained this or am perfect; but I press on to make it my own, because Christ has made me his own. Brethren, I do not consider that I have made it my own; but one thing I do, forgetting what lies behind and straining forward to what lies ahead, I press toward the goal of the upward call of God in Christ Jesus. Let those of us who are mature be like minded; and if in anything you are otherwise minded, God will reveal that also to you. Only let us hold true to what we have attained. (Philippians 3:12-16)

3) *We can define our roles to ourselves and our congregations.* If we don't define our roles, others will do it for us. Part of this defining process requires clergy and spouses to be clear about their expectations of each other. This may take some working through of conflicting expectations, but it will make it possible for the clergy-person and spouse to support each other's role.

Also, if we believe in the shared ministry of the lay and the ordained it is essential that we articulate what the role of clergy is in that shared ministry. If we don't know who we are in the role, or have no theological grounding for it, how can we expect our congregations to know what to expect from us?

4) *We can value ourselves enough to take time for rest, recreation, family, spouse and friends.* This will entail some setting of limits so that ministry will not use up all our time, for surely there are no limits unless *we* set them. One clergyperson who was seeking to keep his time commitments in perspective said, "I will give my family priority. The church could fold tomorrow or they could fire me, but my family I have with me always. This may cause some problems in ministry, but I would rather have those kinds of problems than to have my family fall apart." God calls us to faithful personal and family relationships as well as to faithful ministry in parish relationships. Another clergyperson said he learned that it was not only all right, but actually necessary to take time for *himself* as well as for his relationships with others. He now plans for time to be alone, and time for activities that renew *him*.

How can we find time in the midst of demanding schedules? Certainly it is no easy matter. Part of the solution may be the "secret of a full date book." If we want time for our spouses, family and ourselves, we need to *schedule it*, putting it in our date books well ahead of time. Then when we are asked if we can come to a meeting, we consult our datebooks, and if that time has already been scheduled for family, we say that we are unavailable. Some such approach as this seems essential if we are to keep any kind of balance in our busy lives.

For most of us, the tasks of defining our roles and setting limits are ones that need to be done again and again, for all too quickly the lines become blurred and the people-needs overwhelm us once again.

5) *We can remind ourselves that we don't have to be without the support we need.* There is support available, and from a variety of sources. It seems clear that if we are willing to take initiative and risk sharing our needs with others, we can find adequate support in spite of some of the handicaps that we have talked about. For instance, one clergyman was suffering pain and loneliness after being fired, and didn't know where to turn. He finally realized that he had pastor friends who didn't even know what was happening to him. He got on the phone and contacted them and, as he said, "I got my support." It was important that he had those friendships firmly in place before crisis hit, and that he was willing to take the initiative to ask for what he needed during the crisis.

B. What Issues Need To Be Addressed By Seminaries and Professional Groups?

The profession of ministry is in the midst of change and ferment. Clergy need help in grappling with these changes. Seminaries and professional groups should provide the forum.

   1) *Seminaries and professional groups could do more to help students and ministers define who they are and who they are not.* One's images of ministry, ordination and success usually precede seminary. Unless the seminaries help make visible these images, and challenge or confirm metaphors for ministry both theologically and experientially, individuals may head for the parish poorly equipped to deal with the complexities of ministry today.

   2) *Seminaries and professional groups need to address and encourage the "whole person" in ministry.* Spiritual formation, personal growth and physical well-being as well as academic preparation are theological imperatives. I believe that the minister of the future is being called to model as well as teach a holistic approach. If we believe that the patterns set in seminaries are carried over to parish ministry, then seminaries will need to find ways to model a style of wholeness during the seminary years.

   This might include providing spiritual direction and encouraging students to take seriously their physical well-being. It might even include fostering personal growth by requiring individual or group counseling as part of seminary training. There is a precedent for this. Personal therapy is required in the training of therapists so they might become aware of interpersonal dynamics and work on any issues that might get in the way of their being good therapists. As one pastoral counselor who works with many clergy and spouses said,

> If clergy dealt with their internal person, when they came out of seminary they would be less threatened. The average parish minister deals with a lot of transference, and individual therapy would be a way to help them deal creatively with this transference. We need to work on ourselves. The "me" is one of the chief instruments of ministry.

   3) *Seminaries and professional groups need to counteract the cultural ideal of self-sufficiency and the pressure to act as if "I have it all together."* The cultural patterns need to be theologically chal-

lenged and the Christian counter-cultural patterns need to be modeled in the preparation for ministry. Seminaries could seek new ways to encourage and model interdependence, collegiality and the sharing of vulnerability. The search for excellence in ministry is not the search for perfection, but the creative development of one's gifts as called forth and encouraged by the community.

4) *Seminaries and denominations might consider requiring an intern year before graduation, or a "residency" after graduation.* Currently the Lutheran Church and the Unitarian Universalist Association require an intern year, and the Episcopal Church requires a period of time set aside after seminary and before ordination to the priesthood. During such a period there could be gatherings to reflect on the experience of ministry from within the setting of the parish. Until actually in the parish one may not be asking the right questions or be open to hearing creative answers. Additional options for meeting the challenges of the first years of ministry are dealt with in *Beyond the Boundary* (1986).

5) *During seminary education we need to make more use of the expertise of those persons already in the parish.* Perhaps one of the best practical supports that seminaries and the "in-care process" could provide is to use parish clergy (and spouses of parish clergy) to share their experiences around specific issues. There needs to be flesh and blood testimony that says, "This works for me. It might for you."

6) *There needs to be the development of more continuing education and advanced degree programs that support and challenge the "whole person" in ministry, not just the improvement of knowledge and skills.* For example, as I noted earlier, the Doctor of Ministry program at the Institute for Advanced Pastoral Studies (Detroit, Michigan) fosters prayer as a metaphor for ministry and supports personal growth as the individual grapples with the theological issues which undergird ministry.

As with each of these sections on "possibilities and directions," this raises only a few of the many possibilities and offers no easy answers. However, these directions for the profession and for the seminaries that train clergy seem to be some of the most significant ones in relationship to the issues raised in this book.

C. What Can the Denominational Systems Do to Support Clergy and Their Spouses?

Denominational structures have an investment in the health, well-being and continued growth of clergy and their spouses. There is an intimate connection between the well-being of clergy and the health and well-being of the churches they serve. There is also a connection between the well-being of the spouse and the well-being of the clergyperson. The system cannot and should not try to do for the individuals what they can do for themselves, but there are some changes and support needs which take initiative by the judicatory. Also there are times when individuals are unable to take initiative for themselves or simply need the encouragement and support of others who are there to minister to them. The denominational system can be for clergy and spouses: 1) a permission-giver and question-raiser; 2) a facilitator of networks; 3) an advocate; 4) a cheerleader; and 5) a provider of resources.

1) Permission-Giver and Question-Raiser

As we have seen in previous chapters, many of the things that stand in the way of clergy and spouses receiving the support they need are subtle and internal attitudes and scripts. No amount of programming, in and of itself, will address these needs effectively. As one Conference staff person said, "I'm getting a little cynical about planning things for clergy support. Those who need it don't come." What might break through this impasse? One of the most meaningful roles of Conference leaders could be to serve as "permission-givers." There need to be ways to let clergy and spouses know that it is really all right, and even essential, to seek help.

One Conference staff person who teaches a polity course talks with her students about the need to grow and deal with personal issues during one's ministry. She talks with them about finding counseling resources for doing this, and about their concern for what people in their congregations will think if their minister "has to go for help." But, she doesn't leave it there! She goes on to acknowledge that she herself goes to a counselor who is very helpful and keeps absolute confidentiality. "I'll be glad to give you his number anytime," she adds. By sharing her personal experience, she is saying to them that this is more than something she advocates for others. She is saying, I need this kind of support and I am getting it. That is being a permission-giver!

Another clergyman told me about attending a workshop that helped him grow. How did he happen to attend? His Area Minister

recommended it to him, having attended it himself. As the clergyman said about this experience: "He (the Area Minister) didn't have
it all together, so it was o.k. for me not to have it all together." This
Area Minister was being a permission-giver. When denominational
leaders are willing to share their own humanness with parish
clergy, and witness to how they seek or find their support, clergy
are enabled to discover new possibilities for gaining support also.

Denominational staff are also in a unique position to raise important underlying questions about ministry and script patterns.
Gatherings of clergy provide a forum for some of these underlying
issues to be raised. One Area Minister recently asked a group of
clergy how they were feeling about their support systems. The very
act of raising this question helped some clergy think about a need
that is often swept under the carpet. Some people believe that it
would work better if this question-raiser and facilitator came from
outside the system. In either case, one clergyperson summed it up
when he said, "We need someone who is open, genuine and sharing, and who will help us get started talking about the real issues
that go beyond what we will do for the Thanksgiving service."

Obviously, permission-giving and question-raising regarding
these underlying issues will only happen if denominational staff are
convinced that these are important parts of their ministry to ministers, and if denominational staff have begun to confront some of
these issues in their own lives. It is important to have people in
these positions who have the capacity to elicit humanness in others.
It is in the sharing of our journeys with each other along the way
that we provide each other with the support needed to take the
next steps in personal/spiritual growth.

2) Facilitator of Networks

Denominational staff are too busy to provide all the support clergy
and spouses need or might like. This is especially true in Conferences such as Massachusetts where an Area Minister is responsible
for pastoring more than 150 clergy in addition to programming and
settlement responsibilities. They simply cannot be personally available to so many. The most frequent suggestion from UCC clergy in
both Massachusetts and Iowa was that it would be helpful if Conferences would provide a "pastor to pastors" who has no responsibility
for either placement or the local church. The Michigan Conference
has provided such a person, and it has worked well. The three
counselors available in the Pennsylvania UCC Conferences are another significant attempt to address the problem of providing support personnel who are not involved in placement. In a UCC

Conference such as Massachusetts, having a pastor to the pastors would be a useful supplement to the Area Minister's work, but it would be no panacea. This is such a large Conference that it would require more than one person to touch base with all the clergy. Additional approaches must be found to build adequate support in large Conferences.

Though the word "networking" is a bit overused, the concept suggests a creative direction for the Conference as it tries to address what it can do to support clergy and spouses. The aim of networking is to extend the range of individual and group supports.

How might the Conference help expand the individual and group supports? Before making a proposal in response to this question, let me first review some of the clergy and spouse issues that have been identified previously, and to which my proposal speaks.

a) There is generally a low level of collegial support for both clergy and spouses.

b) Clergy and spouses need support from persons in similar circumstances.

c) Good support groups for clergy or clergy couples clearly provide important sources of support and growth, yet there are relatively few such groups.

d) Spouses of clergy have little connection with each other.

e) Many clergy have difficulty moving beyond competitive shop-talk to deeper relationship.

f) There are certain key issues and stages in a clergyperson's career where there are special needs.

g) Clergy and spouses have limited time and money, both of which prevent or inhibit their attendance at workshops and seminars.

h) Currently, many Conferences gather large groups of clergy for excellent one-day programs focused on stress, retirement or other issues, but most of these are one-shot programs with little encouragement for ongoing collegiality or support.

i) These workshops are usually led by outside "experts" and, as several clergy pointed out, if you happen to miss the stress workshop because of a schedule conflict, you have lost your chance.

Keeping these factors in mind, is there anything the Conference could do to "minister to the ministers" and at the same time encourage collegial support?

The Conference could identify key clergy and spouses within the Conference who have dealt with, or are dealing with, specific life or ministry issues and situations such as these: first parish; being an associate minister; spiritual renewal; transitions from one church to another; mid-life issues; dealing with grief in oneself or within the parish; clergy divorce; retirement; coping with the pressures on clergy marriages; negotiating our roles with our congregations; stress; time-problems in ministry; long pastorate; conflict in the parish; etc. These selected persons might be given financial support to attend workshops or seminars which would further clarify the issue they were dealing with (e.g. Alban Institute's "Long Pastorate," or "Clergy Divorce," or "Pastoral Start-Up," or "Clergy Self-Evaluation.") These clergy or spouses would, in turn, agree to lead two or three small groups of clergy and/or spouses within the Conference over a two-year period. These groups would be formed by specific and general invitation. For example, I envision a letter going out from one of these leaders to persons 40-50 years of age saying something like this:

> Are you finding that certain questions about life and ministry seem to be surfacing at this point in your life? (At this point I would list some of the questions.) These kinds of questions have surfaced for me, and because of them I recently went to a mid-life seminar at Kirkridge Conference Center. I found it extremely helpful. I also became aware of how good it was to share some of these issues with my peers in the ministry. Therefore, with the Conference's blessing, I am writing to invite you to meet with me for——(two days or 4 Monday nights, or whatever). I look forward to the kind of sharing we can do with each other, but there will be no pressure to share more than you are ready to. I believe that we can learn from each other.

Similar letters could be sent to identified groups focussed around other issues.

The persons chosen for this kind of leadership would need to have two characteristics. First, they would need to have personal experience with the particular issue around which the group would be formed, along with a high degree of willingness to share their own experience. Secondly, they would need to have some group skills and would need to come as leader/participant, not as the person with all the answers.

In order to free up time for clergy to provide this leadership, the Conference might release clergy from Sunday responsibilities by providing pulpit-supply. Perhaps a group of retired clergy might be willing to do this.

What would be the values of an approach like this? To name a few:

a) It supports, honors, and develops leadership within the Conference.

b) It moves toward clergy supporting clergy rather than always looking to "experts."

c) It supports collegial relationship of clergy in small groups, which might lead to some ongoing supportive relationships.

d) It allows groups to be held in local areas and therefore would be available for little or no cost.

e) It enables a particular issue to be dealt with repeatedly, not only on a one-shot basis.

f) It is a permission-giving process, especially if the leaders are willing to be open to sharing their own experience.

g) It encourages interdependence rather than dependence or independence.

h) It promotes a model of "becoming" rather than "arrival."

A number of clergy said that one of the things that the Conference could do best to support them would be to bring them together so that relationships might develop. The above proposal is made with the belief that to gain full value from this coming together, groups need, first, to be focussed on something that is of current importance to their members; second, the groups need to be small; and, third they need a format that can move the sharing to a deeper level.

I do not believe that in most cases any outside group or leader can set up clergy or spouse *ongoing* peer support groups. There are too many intangible and personality issues involved in whether a certain group of people will jell into a good support group. However, if the Conference can facilitate small groups around personal or ministerial issues, in the process the individuals will form bonds that are far more important than the issues themselves.

Where leadership is needed or desired, pastoral counselors might be used to provide it. They come with special skills and parish experience and are often an under-used resource. The Conference might facilitate small collegial groups by identifying pastoral counselors who are willing to provide such leadership.

There is one other specific action that I believe is worth considering at a Conference level. The first year or two in the parish is known to be one of the highest stress times in ministry, and is also a time when ministry patterns are developed. One person who works with clergy indicated that he is seeing too many new pastors get "chewed up in their first parishes and leave the ministry or end up totally demoralized." A *mentor network* is one creative way of supporting clergy and spouses during this period. A system of mentors is working well for clergy in Nebraska (Kreml, 1982, p. 35). A new pastor is paired with a mentor who is selected by the Conference because of his/her ability to listen, to be sensitive to the needs and concerns of pastors and their families, and to confront when necessary. The mentor has also demonstrated success in local church relations and parish ministry. The new pastor and the mentor meet regularly to touch base on issues that have surfaced for the new pastor. What is shared in these meetings is confidential between the two persons. This is a very significant way to gain support and keep perspective during this crucial period. Since this is also a particularly difficult time for spouses, I believe that there should be ways of including them in this process. (See also suggestions in Harbaugh, et al, 1986.)

3) Advocate

One of the ways that the denominational offices support clergy is by preparing and sending salary guidelines to the churches, procedures for seeking placement in new churches, etc. They can also support clergy by negotiating the best possible health insurance plan.

Another key point where clergy need an advocate is when they are considering leaving or have decided to leave the parish ministry. There seems to be no way to exit from the parish ministry gracefully. Frequently, it is interpreted as a denial of one's call from God in favor of the secular world. These clergy often feel judged and consider themselves failures. (Even some clergy who have left the parish to serve as pastoral counselors, though still intentionally functioning in a pastoral role, have felt excluded from the ranks of ministry.) For whatever reason clergy leave the parish ministry they need advocates and support in the midst of this transition. They need to know that the church honors ministry in the world as well as ministry in the church.

4) Cheerleader

Most people grow and thrive best with plenty of affirmation. When this affirmation comes from people in the denominational structure it often has strong impact. We all need "cheerleaders," and sometimes the ministry has very few. Here are a few illustrations of ways in which the denominational staff can be a cheerleader for clergy and spouses.

a) Find ways to acknowledge creative and faithful ministry. Sometimes recognition seems limited to successful church growth or mission-giving. While these kinds of success are to be honored and shared, it is important that we guard against seeing success in ministry only in terms of our cultural standards, e.g. bigger, better, more efficient. We need to ask ourselves what is the theological base for measuring "success" in ministry, and then find ways (even quiet ways) of sharing stories, which though less dramatic, are equally faithful.

b) When a Conference staff person visits the local church, his/her active listening and interest in what is happening in that local church and in the lives of the clergyperson and spouse is a form of cheerleading.

c) Finding ways to keep in contact with clergy on a reasonably regular basis is another way to demonstrate that Conference personnel are caring and cheering clergy on. This might be done by a phone call or a note or a recognition of a special occasion.

d) Inviting clergy spouses to gatherings such as those held for new ministers is one way of saying that "we know you are involved, too." The Conference could use such times to plan programs that treat spouses as individuals, not just as appendages to clergy, and at the same time acknowledge that ministry greatly impacts the lives of spouses. For instance, it might be important to use the time with spouses to address ways of clarifying and negotiating their role with the congregation. This says to spouses that the denomination knows they have some important issues to deal with, and whatever role they choose in the church, it is important.

5) Provider of Resources

All of the Conferences I contacted are trying to provide resources for clergy. This is done through *people, programs* and *funding* for special needs. All are important. I will not try to enumerate the many kinds of programs, workshops, retreats, etc. that are offered. Rather I will focus on four issues:

a) Having both *resources and funds available for counseling* is essential. Since Conference funds for counseling are frequently inadequate, one Conference came up with the creative idea of taking a collection at all installations and ordinations, using this money to support clergy in counseling and continuing education. Also people need to be able to get access to these funds without going through Conference personnel who are involved in placement. This is true for other than monetary resources. The Massachusetts Conference of the UCC provides a phone number for clergy to call if they are having a problem with alcohol. However, they need to go through the Conference office to get this phone number. Some individuals are unwilling to contact the Conference office to get the number. Spouses also need referrals that feel safe. I talked with two clergy spouses who have an alcohol problem, and who feel that it is more difficult for them to ask for help because of their husband's clergy position. The Connecticut UCC Conference is attempting to circumvent this problem by providing direct and confidential access to help.

b) Many clergy and spouses are unaware of the resources available to support them. Therefore, it would be helpful to have a *booklet that lists the available resources and how to reach them*, along with a permission-giving statement about our common need for support. This might include a listing of pastoral counseling centers, funds available, and the many other Conference and personal resources. I would suggest that a copy of this booklet, along with a separate letter, be sent to all spouses of clergy as well as to clergy. This is one way to say to the spouses that we care for them also, and that the Conference realizes resources for support are important.

c) *Send materials to clergy and spouses at specific transition points*. One clergyperson suggested a unique way for Conference personnel to provide resources and support. He said that there are some excellent booklets about starting in a new parish, terminating a pastorate, etc. When a clergyperson is going through a transition of this kind, it would be both helpful and supportive if a Conference person sent him one of these resources with a letter indicating that he/she would be available for further conversation if it was desired.

d) Finally, another way in which Conferences could be both a provider of resources and cheerleader is *by providing economical ways for clergy and their spouses to have time away together*. For example, the Massachusetts Conference makes lodging at Craigville Conference Center available at very reasonable rates, even at no cost on occasion. The Nebraska Conference provides

"Mini-holidays" for clergy and spouses where housing is provided at a college, camp or motel. In a slightly different vein, the Connecticut Conference provides Ingraham House, a center where clergy can go on individual retreat, and which includes two apartments to house clergy families if they have to leave their church and have no other place to live. For those clergy on very tight budgets and in difficult circumstances these are major supportive efforts by Conferences.

In conclusion, it is clear there are numerous ways to increase the quantity and quality of support. It is also clear that clergy and spouses have to assume the primary responsibility of developing their own supports. However, the denominational structures *do* have a major role to play in enabling this to happen. Conferences or other judicatories have an investment in the well-being of clergy and their spouses. They can foster wholeness in ministry by the "permissions" they give, the questions they raise, the networks they facilitate and the resources they provide. They can be an advocate for their clergy by being a bridge to the national agencies and churches. And they can cheer clergy and spouses on through affirmation and signs of caring. Seminaries can help clergy with the issue of support by alerting them to some of the pitfalls of ministry, advocating and modeling a holistic approach to ministry and helping students address some of the key issues and questions of ministry before those ministries actually begin. Only as the individual, the seminary and the denominational structures all address the need for support will we see significant changes take place.

Epilogue

There was one major surprise that came out of this study. When I set out to request interviews with clergy and their spouses at the beginning of this project, I felt apologetic. After all, I was asking for two hours of busy people's time. I felt I was imposing on them. My initial requests were responded to graciously. Some people hearing of my study even volunteered to be interviewed. The real surprise was how many people were eager to talk about themselves and their experiences in ministry. At the conclusion of the interviews the vast majority of the people expressed gratitude for my listening to their stories. Several even invited me to come back again if I wanted to explore other issues. Clearly, there was a *need* on their part to talk and to be heard. Some found that the interview helped them focus on the issue of support in some new ways and gave them fresh clarity. For some of the people interviewed this was the first time anyone had asked them about how they got their support, and my asking them was, in itself, a form of support. The process was aided by the fact that I promised confidentiality, and therefore I was a "safe person." All of these factors helped make this a good experience for me, and for many of the persons I interviewed.

It was a rare privilege to talk with this wonderful variety of people with all their joys and pains, with all their uniqueness, humanness, and their desire to be faithful to what they believe. I am grateful for their sharing and I learned much from them. It reconfirmed in me the need for us all to listen to each other's stories. This may be one of the greatest gifts we can give each other!

Bellah, Robert N., Richard Madsen, William Sullivan, Ann Swidler and Steven Tipton, *Habits of the Heart*, Berkeley: University of California Press, 1985.

Bible, The, Revised Standard Version, Old Testament 1952, New Testament 1946, New York: Thomas Nelson and Sons.

Biersdorf, John E., *Healing of Purpose*, Nashville: Abingdon, 1985.

Brueggmann, Walter, "Covenant as a Subversive Paradigm," *The Christian Century*, Nov. 12, 1980, p. 1095.

Bush, Bernard J. and Thomas A. Kane, *Coping: Issues of Emotional Living in an Age of Stress for Clergy and Religious*, Whitinsville, Massachusetts: Affirmation Books, 1976.

Clergy in Crisis Report to the General Synod XV, United Church of Christ, New York: Office of Church Life and Leadership, 1985.

Clergy Morale Study, *Church Leaders' Bulletin*, United Church of Christ, Spring 1982.

Coger, Marian, *Women in Parish Ministry: Stress and Support*, Washington, DC: The Alban Institute, Inc., 1985.

Douglas, William, *Ministers Wives*, New York: Harper and Row, 1965.

Douglass, Bruce G. and Clark Moustakas, "Heuristic Inquiry: The Internal Search to Know," *The Journal of Humanistic Psychology*, Vol. 25, No.3, Summer 1985, pp. 35-55.

Edwards, Tilden, "The Spiritual Life of the Pastor," *Action Information*, Washington, DC: The Alban Institute, Inc., Mar.-Apr. 1985, p. 6.

Ellison, Craig W., Ed., *Your Better Self, Christianity, Psychology and Self-Esteem*, San Francisco: Harper and Row, 1983.

Erickson, Erik H., *Insight and Responsibility*, New York: W. W. Norton, 1964.

Fenhagen, James C., *Mutual Ministry*, New York: Seabury Press, 1977.

———, *Ministry and Solitude*, New York: Seabury Press, 1981.

Fletcher, John, *Religious Authenticity in the Clergy*, Washington, DC: Alban Institute, Inc., 1979.

Friedman, Edwin H., *Generation to Generation, Family Process in Church and Synagogue*, New York: The Guilford Press, 1985.

Gilbert, Barbara G., "Personality Type and the Spiritual Journey," *Haelan*, Detroit: Institute for Advanced Pastoral Studies, Winter 1984-85, pp. 4-15.

Gilligan, Carol, *In a Different Voice*, Cambridge, MA: Harvard University Press, 1982.

Hahn, Celia A. and James R. Adams, *The Mystery of Clergy Authority*, Washington, DC: The Alban Institute, Inc. 1980.

Harbaugh, Gary L. and Evan Rogers, "Pastoral Burnout: A View From the Seminary," *The Journal of Pastoral Care*, Vol. XXXVIII, No. 2, 1984.

Harbaugh, Gary L., William C. Behrens, Jill M. Hudson and Roy M. Oswald, *Beyond the Boundary*, Washington, DC: The Alban Institute, Inc., 1986.

Harris, John C., *Stress, Power and Ministry*, Washington, DC: The Alban Institute, Inc., 1982.

Hartley, Loyde H., *A Study of Clergy Morale*, Lancaster, PA: Research Center in Religion and Society, Lancaster Theological Seminary, 1980.

Henderson, Holly, *My Pastor Has a Family*, New York: Office of Church Life and Leadership, United Church of Christ, 1976.

James, Muriel and Dorothy Jongeward, *Born to Win*, Reading, MA: Addison- Wesley, 1971.

Kemper, Robert G., *What Every Church Member Should Know About Clergy*, New York: Pilgrim Press, 1985.

Kreml, Anne Lee, *Pastoral Care of Pastors and Their Families*, Nebraska Conference of the United Church of Christ, unpublished manuscript, April 1982.

Larson, Bruce, "None of Us Are Sinners Emeritus," *Leadership Magazine*, Vol.V, No.4, Fall 1984, pp. 12-23.

Leavitt, Daniel B., *A Faith for the Middle Years*, Washington, DC: The Alban Institute, Inc., 1982.

Levinson, Daniel J., *Seasons of a Man's Life*, New York: Knopf, 1978.

Mace, David and Vera Mace, *What's Happening to Clergy Marriages?*, Nashville: Abingdon, 1980.

McClelland, David C., *Power: The Inner Experience*, New York: Irvington, 1975.

McFague, Sallie, *Metaphorical Theology*, Philadelphia: Fortress Press, 1982.

Merrill, Dean, *Clergy Couples in Crisis*, Waco, TX: Word Books, 1985.

Mills, Edgar W. and John P. Koval, *Stress in the Ministry*, Ministry Studies Board, 1717 Massachusetts Ave. NW, Washington, DC 20036, 1971, An IDOC Document.

Nouwen, Henri J.M., *Intimacy*, San Francisco: Harper and Row, 1969.

———— *Creative Ministry*, Garden City, N.Y.: Doubleday and Company, 1971.

———— *The Wounder Healer*, Garden City, N.Y.: Doubleday, 1972.

Oswald, Roy M., "The Vulnerability of Clergy," *Action Information*, Washington, DC: The Alban Institute, Inc., Nov.-Dec. 1981, pp. 5-7.

———— *Clergy Stress and Burnout*, Funded and Prepared by Ministers Life Resources, Inc., Minneapolis, MN, 1982.

———— "Why Do Clergy Wives Burn Out?," *Action Information*, Washington, DC: The Alban Institute, Jan.-Feb. 1984, pp.11-15.

Oswald, Roy M., Carolyn Gutierrez, and Liz Dean, *Married to the Minister*, Washington, DC: The Alban Institute, Inc., 1980.

Oswald, Roy M., Gail D. Hinand, William Chris Hobgood and Barton M. Lloyd, *New Visions for the Long Pastorate*, Washington, DC: The Alban Institute, Inc., 1983.

Palmer, Parker, "Borne Again," *The Auburn News*, New York: Auburn Theological Seminary, Fall 1985.

Professional Ethics Group, *Intimacy in the Parish*, Preliminary Grant Report: Grant #840205, Center for Ethics and Social Policy, Graduate Theological Union, California, July 1, 1985.

Reed, Bruce, *The Task of the Church and the Role of its Members*, The Grubb Institute, 1975, Reprinted with permission by the Alban Institute, Inc. in 1984.

Reid, Clyde, *The Return to Faith*, New York: Harper and Row, 1974.

Sanford, John A., *Ministry Burnout*, New York/Ramsey: The Paulist Press, 1982.

Satir, Virginia, *People Making*, Palo Alto, California: Science and Behavior Books, Inc., 1972.

Sheehey, Gail, *Passages*, New York: E.P. Dutton, 1972.

———— *Pathfinders*, New York: William Morrow, 1981.

Spitz, Rene, "Hospitalism: Genesis of Psychiatric Conditions in Early Childhood," *Psychoanalytic Study of the Child*, (1:53-71), 1945.

Steiner, Claude, *Scripts People Live*, New York: Grove Press, 1974.

Strong, David, *Who Ministers to the Minister?*, D. Min. Dissertation, The Institute for Advanced Pastoral Studies, 8425 W. McNichols Road, Detroit, MI 48221, 1983.

Tracy, Bruce, "Student Concerns, Integration, Balance and Support," *Today's Ministry*, Newton, MA: Andover Newton Theological School, Vol. II, No. 2, Winter 1985, p. 110.

Weidman, Judith L., Ed., *Christian Feminism*, San Francisco: Harper and Row, 1984.

Whybrew, Lyndon E., *Minister, Wife and Church: Unlocking the Triangle*, Washington, DC: The Alban Institute, Inc., 1984.

Winslow, Donald, *The Ministry of Jesus*. A sermon at Episcopal Theological Seminary in Cambridge, MA, January 1979.

Zikmund, Barbara Brown, Dean of Pacific School of Religion, *Between Office and Profession*, Lectures at the Pastors Study Conference, Springfield, MA, February 1986.

Research Design, Scope and Process

The major sources of data for this study are as follows:

1) A Questionnaire

The study began with the development of a questionnaire to gather preliminary data. (Questionnaire and results are in Appendices II-VIII.) The first purpose of this questionnaire was to learn how clergy and clergy spouses felt about the availability of support. I wanted to know whether or not they found it hard to find persons to talk with about personal issues and whether or not they were hesitant to ask for help. I wanted to check their perceptions of whether they felt there were adequate available resources in denominational structures to minister to their needs. (Appendix III)

The second purpose of the questionnaire was to gather data regarding personal issues and where they found support when dealing with them. The data is in Appendices IV-VIII, and is referred to throughout this manuscript.

Initially the questionnaire was distributed to clergy and spouses of clergy at the Annual Meeting of the Massachusetts Conference of the United Church of Christ in June, 1985. Lay delegates were encouraged to take questionnaires to clergy and spouses who were not in attendance. One hundred and fifty-one questionnaires were completed and returned to me. Smaller samples were obtained from UCC clergy and spouses in other Conferences and from a small group of clergy and spouses of other mainline denominations—Methodist, Episcopal, Southern Baptist, Baptist, Presbyterian, Christian Church-Disciples of Christ.

A second major sample was taken in Iowa. The Iowa Conference of the United Church of Christ distributed the questionnaire to all clergy and spouses asking that it be filled out and returned to me. Sixty-seven responses were received. My aim was to check out responses in another geographical area.

2) Clergy and clergy spouse interviews

The findings from the questionnaire were preliminary data for the research project. The heart of my research was the interviews I conducted with 47 UCC clergy and spouses. Thirty-nine of these were from Massachusetts and eight from California and New Hampshire. Each of these interviews were 1 1/2-2 hours long. The individuals were selected to represent a distribution in age, church size and location (rural, urban, suburban, town). The sample included 8 female clergy, 22 male clergy, 14 female spouses, 3 male spouses. There were married, divorced, single and homosexual clergy represented.

The method of interview was based on a heuristic research model (Douglass, Bruce G. & Moustakas, Clark, 1985, pp. 39-55), aimed at uncovering the *meaning* and *essence* behind the individual's experience of seeking to find support for personal issues. As a researcher using this method of study, I could allow myself to become involved in the interview process, occasionally sharing some personal experience or data as a "touchstone" to help elicit their similar or dissimilar experience. In each interview I asked for a "critical incident" in their lives when they especially needed support, and asked them to identify how they received that support. (Sample questions in Appendix IX)

Because there was no opportunity to interview the Iowa sample face to face, I included six interview questions that individuals could respond to in writing. In addition to these individual interviews, I had the opportunity for a group interview with 8 clergy representing Baptist, Methodist, Episcopal and the United Church of Christ denominations.

3) Data from persons who work with clergy

In search of answers from a slightly different perspective, I sought out individuals who work professionally with clergy and clergy spouses. I conducted 18 personal interviews and had phone conversations or correspondence with 16 additional persons. These included: UCC Conference and Area Ministers in 8 states; a Pastoral Counselor and a Career Development Counselor, both of whom see many clergy; a seminary professor, administrators, deans and students from 4 seminaries; a person who is working to provide networks for clergy with alcohol problems; the head of a church outreach agency who works with many clergy and has concern for clergy-support; and a person who is seeking to provide networking for clergy spouses.

The clergy, spouses, and persons working with clergy, who participated in this part of the research were told how I would use the data I was gathering. All interviews were taped. They agreed to have their stories told and these stories are an integral part of this project. I promised confidentiality and therefore have altered the details so that no individual could be identified. Whenever quotes appear that do not have acknowledgment, they come from one of my interviewees.

4) Other studies and research

Finally, I sought out other research and writings in the area of support-needs and systems. I am indebted to those who have explored many facets of these issues, and I have listed the most important ones in the references.

You will note that I have limited my research mainly to clergy and spouses of clergy in the United Church of Christ. Only a small sample of questionnaires and the one ecumenical group-interview gathered information from other mainline denominations. I discovered few differences in my data between the UCC and these other denominations, but I consider the sample too small to provide any valid comparison. Beyond my own data, studies and writings from other denominations indicate that the issues and needs are the same, though there are some variations in how each judicatory responds to them.

Though the major part of my research is limited to the United Church of Christ, I believe that it is applicable to clergy and clergy spouses in all the major denominations.

Sample Questionnaire

Denomination _____ State _____

Circle all of the following words that pertain to you:

A. Personal data: Male   Female   Married   Single
    Currently or previously divorced   Ordained clergy   Spouse of clergy

B. Location of present parish: town   suburban   small city   large city

Circle the figure that comes closest to:

C. Number of years in parish ministry (to be answered by clergy)
    1 5 10 15 20 25 30 35 40 45 50

Number of years married to parish minister (to be answered by spouses)
    1 5 10 15 20 25 30 35 40 45 50

D. Your Age: 20 25 30 35 40 45 50 55 60 65 70 75 80

E. Number of years in present parish: 1 5 10 15 20 25 30

F. Membership of present church: Under 100 100-250 250-400 400-550
    550-700 700-850 850-1000 over 1000

Based on your personal experience with issues such as stress or burnout, marital issues, spiritual dryness, conflict in parish, depression, personal crisis of any kind: (Check the box that corresponds to your feelings. Both clergy and spouses answer all 5 questions.)

	Strongly Agree	Moderately Agree	Uncertain	Moderately Disagree	Strongly Disagree
1. Clergy often have difficulty finding persons to talk with when they need support for personal issues.					
2. Spouses of clergy often have difficulty finding persons to talk with when they need support for personal issues.					
3. Clergy are hesitant to ask for help when they need it.					
4. Spouses of clergy are hesitant to ask for help when they need it.					
5. There are adequate resources in our denominational structures to provide the support we need for personal issues.					

APPENDIX II (cont.)

I. Which of the personal issues listed below have been part of your life during your time as a parish minister or being married to a parish minister? (These could be either long or short term issues)

Circle the number preceding the issue.

II. When you were involved in the issues that you circled, to whom did you turn? With whom did you talk about your concern?
a. First check all persons you turned to for support for each of your issues. (If you talked to no one, check that box.)
b. Then go back and circle Ⓥ the check marks of those persons who provided the most significant support.

	No one	Other (please name)	Support Group	God through prayer and meditation	Spiritual Director or Guide	Fellow clergy or spouse of clergy	Pastoral Counselor	Secular therapist	Area or Conference Minister of UCC	Parishioners	Friends (not in parish)	Spouse
1. Depression												
2. Spiritual Dryness												
3. Marital or Sexual Problems												
4. Uncertainty about whether to stay in parish ministry												
5. Feelings of being trapped or stuck												
6. Substance abuse (drugs or alcohol)												
7. High Stress or "burn-out"												
8. Major conflict with parishioners or staff												
9. Family problems (children, parents, in-laws)												
10. Serious concern over health (yours or family)												
11. Serious concern about financial problems												

Data Summary of First Page of Questionnaire

CLERGY—149 respondents (30-female, 119-male)
Major sample from Massachusetts and Iowa, with a small sample from miscellaneous states.

	Strongly Agree	Moderately Agree	Uncertain	Moderately Disagree	Strongly Disagree
1. Clergy often have difficulty finding persons to talk with when they need support for personal issues.	112 *		1	36	
2. Spouses of clergy often have difficulty finding persons to talk with when they need support for personal issues.	107		13	17	
3. Clergy are hesitant to ask for help when they need it.	126		5	18	
4. Spouses of clergy are hesitant to ask for help when they need it.	101		16	11	
5. There are adequate resources in our denominational structures to provide the support we need for personal issues. **	36		35	74	

SPOUSES OF CLERGY—81 respondents (72-female, 9-male)
Major sample from Iowa and Massachusetts. Small sample from other states.

	Strongly Agree	Moderately Agree	Uncertain	Moderately Disagree	Strongly Disagree
1. Clergy often have difficulty finding persons to talk with when they need support for personal issues.	57 *		1	18	
2. Spouses of clergy often have difficulty finding persons to talk with when they need support for personal issues.	63		1	14	
3. Clergy are hesitant to ask for help when they need it.	59		7	8	
4. Spouses of clergy are hesitant to ask for help when they need it.	63		3	12	
5. There are adequate resources in our denominational structures to provide the support we need for personal issues. **	16		27	39	

* In order to give a quick, over-all picture, I have combined both responses on the "agree side" and both responses on the "disagree side".

** The numbers do not add up to the total respondents, because a few questions were left unanswered.

APPENDIX IV

CLERGY SAMPLE—149 respondents (30-female, 119-male)

Circled numbers to the left of the issues below indicate that ½ or more of the respondents checked this issue.

The figures in each box below indicate the number of clergy who turned to these persons. Shaded boxes indicate that ½ or more of the persons checking this issue turned to these sources of support.

Issue	No. of persons checking this issue	Spouse	Friends (not in parish)	Parishioners	Area or Conference Minister of UCC	Secular therapist	Pastoral Counselor	Fellow clergy or spouse of clergy	Spiritual Director or Guide	God through prayer and meditation	Support Group	Other (please name)	No one
1. Depression	(89)	67	45	21	20	24	17	42	7	64	34	5	0
2. Spiritual Dryness	(90)	40	20	16	10	2	5	5	15	73	32	5	3
3. Marital or Sexual Problems	(77)	49	14	8	7	30	21	17	3	40	12	2	1
4. Uncertainty about whether to stay in parish ministry	68	50	29	9	25	7	10	38	4	37	15	4	5
5. Feelings of being trapped or stuck	63	51	27	6	26	7	9	27	5	30	21	5	1
6. Substance abuse (drugs or alcohol)	11	5	1	0	1	0	1	0	1	2	3	3	2
7. High Stress or "burn-out"	74	51	25	22	32	11	12	34	4	37	21	4	3
8. Major conflict with parishioners or staff	(79)	63	33	46	56	9	12	41	7	43	17	5	0
9. Family problems (children, parents, in-laws)	41	33	10	13	7	10	9	15	0	26	9	4	0
10. Serious concern over health (yours or family)	45	30	11	12	15	7	1	11	2	27	8	3	0
11. Serious concern about financial problems	56	45	11	16	18	2	4	24	0	20	7	4	3
Total checks—		494	226	169	191	111	100	295	46	400	180	48	18

APPENDIX V

SPOUSES OF CLERGY—81 respondents (72-female) (9-male)

Circled numbers to the left of the issues below indicate that ½ or more of the respondents checked this issue.

The figures in each box below indicate the number of spouses who turned to these persons. Shaded boxes indicate that ½ or more of the persons checking this issue turned to these sources of support.

No. of persons checking this issue	Issue	Spouse	Friends (not in parish)	Parishioners	Area or Conference Minister of UCC	Secular therapist	Pastoral Counselor	Fellow clergy or spouse of clergy	Spiritual Director or Guide	God through prayer and meditation	Support Group	Other (please name)	No one
(58)	1. Depression	44	21	9	2	18	6	17	0	35	8	5	1
31	2. Spiritual Dryness	14	5	4	0	0	0	3	4	15	2	1	9
30	3. Marital or Sexual Problems	21	7	2	2	7	6	3	2	11	2	3	4
18	4. Uncertainty about whether to stay in parish ministry	15	8	2	3	3	1	4	0	7	1	1	3
(42)	5. Feelings of being trapped or stuck	29	8	1	2	4	2	12	0	15	5	3	6
7	6. Substance abuse (drugs or alcohol)	3	1	0	0	3	0	0	0	2	2	0	1
28	7. High Stress or "burn-out"	22	12	7	3	6	0	14	0	12	7	4	1
22	8. Major conflict with parishioners or staff	19	8	4	9	1	0	5	0	10	0	3	2
32	9. Family problems (children, parents, in-laws)	24	16	6	1	9	2	9	0	14	3	6	0
30	10. Serious concern over health (yours or family)	22	11	6	2	2	2	8	1	17	3	8	2
(40)	11. Serious concern about financial problems	30	5	2	2	2	0	6	0	17	1	5	7
	Total checks—	243	102	43	26	55	18	81	7	148	34	40	36

APPENDIX VI

MASSACHUSETTS MALE CLERGY—82 respondents

Circled numbers to the left of the issues below indicate that ½ or more of the respondents checked this issue.

The figures in each box below indicate the number of male clergy who turned to these persons. Shaded boxes indicate that ½ or more of the persons checking this issue turned to these sources of support.

No. of persons checking this issue	Spouse	Friends (not in parish)	Parishioners	Area or Conference Minister of UCC	Secular therapist	Pastoral Counselor	Fellow clergy or spouse of clergy	Spiritual Director or Guide	God through prayer and meditation	Support Group	Other (please name)	No one
(49) 1. Depression	43	25	12	11	13	12	23	5	38	19	4	
(58) 2. Spiritual Dryness	28	14	10	4	1	5	30	11	43	24	2	
(43) 3. Marital or Sexual Problems	27	6	2	5	21	13	7	2	23	8	2	
(45) 4. Uncertainty about whether to stay in parish ministry	38	18	3	20	5	8	26	3	25	11	3	1
(43) 5. Feelings of being trapped or stuck	38	17	3	16	5	7	20	2	23	13	2	
6 6. Substance abuse (drugs or alcohol)	3	1	0	0	0	0	0	0	1	1	1	1
(43) 7. High Stress or "burn-out"	37	15	12	14	7	8	22	3	23	15	3	
(44) 8. Major conflict with parishioners or staff	39	18	27	27	5	10	20	4	24	9	2	
27 9. Family problems (children, parents, in-laws)	24	5	9	4	8	5	9	0	14	6	3	
27 10. Serious concern over health (yours or family)	24	7	8	11	5	1	6	2	17	6	3	
35 11. Serious concern about financial problems	32	8	12	14	2	1	17	0	11	4	1	2
Total checks—	333	134	98	116	72	70	180	32	242	116	26	4

APPENDIX VII

MASSACHUSETTS FEMALE CLERGY—24 respondents

The figures in each box below indicate the number of female clergy who turned to these persons. Shaded boxes indicate that ½ or more of the persons checking this issue turned to these sources of support.

Circled numbers to the left of the issues below indicate that ½ or more of the respondents checked this issue.

No. of persons checking this issue

Issue	No. checking	Spouse	Friends (not in parish)	Parishioners	Area or Conference Minister of UCC	Secular therapist	Pastoral Counselor	Fellow clergy or spouse of clergy	Spiritual Director or Guide	God through prayer and meditation	Support Group	Other (please name)	No one
1. Depression	(16)	9	9	4	3	5	2	8	1	12	6	1	
2. Spiritual Dryness	(13)	5	2	3	0	1	0	4	3	9	1	1	1
3. Marital or Sexual Problems	(13)	9	6	2	1	5	2	3	1	7	2		
4. Uncertainty about whether to stay in parish ministry	8	4	5	4	1	2	1	6	1	5	1		
5. Feelings of being trapped or stuck	10	6	7	2	5	2	1	5	2	5	4		
6. Substance abuse (drugs or alcohol)	3	1	0	0	0	0	1	0	1	0	1	2	
7. High Stress or "burn-out"	(14)	7	8	5	3	2	2	5	1	7	3		
8. Major conflict with parishioners or staff	(14)	10	9	7	9	1	1	8	3	9	4	2	
9. Family problems (children, parents, in-laws)	6	5	2	1	0	2	2	1	0	5	1		
10. Serious concern over health (yours or family)	5	4	1	1	2	1	0	1	0	4	0	3	
11. Serious concern about financial problems	7	5	2	2	2	0	1	3	0	3	1	2	1
Total checks—		65	51	31	26	22	12	45	11	67	25	13	

MASSACHUSETTS FEMALE SPOUSES OF CLERGY—45 respondents

Circled numbers to the left of the issues below indicate that ½ or more of the respondents checked this issue.

The figures in each box below indicate the number of female spouses who turned to these persons. Shaded boxes indicate that ½ or more of the persons checking this issue turned to these sources of support.

No. of persons checking this issue	Issue	Spouse	Friends (not in parish)	Parishioners	Area or Conference Minister of UCC	Secular therapist	Pastoral Counselor	Fellow clergy or spouse of clergy	Spiritual Director or Guide	God through prayer and meditation	Support Group	Other (please name)	No one
36	1. Depression	29	15	7	2	14	5	11	0	24	5	3	1
20	2. Spiritual Dryness	10	4	3	0	0	0	2	2	8	2	0	7
18	3. Marital or Sexual Problems	17	5	1	1	5	5	3	1	8	1	1	0
11	4. Uncertainty about whether to stay in parish ministry	10	5	2	3	2	1	4	0	6	1	1	1
24	5. Feelings of being trapped or stuck	18	4	1	1	3	1	6	0	7	2	2	3
4	6. Substance abuse (drugs or alcohol)	2	1	0	0	2	0	0	0	2	1	0	1
19	7. High Stress or "burn-out"	15	7	4	2	6	0	10	0	9	6	3	1
15	8. Major conflict with parishioners or staff	13	7	3	6	0	0	4	0	7	0	2	1
22	9. Family problems (children, parents, in-laws)	18	12	4	0	6	2	4	0	10	3	5	0
19	10. Serious concern over health (yours or family)	13	6	4	1	1	1	4	1	12	2	6	2
24	11. Serious concern about financial problems	18	4	2	2	2	0	5	0	10	1	3	5
	Total checks—	163	70	31	18	41	15	53	4	103	24	26	22

Interviews—Questions Asked of Clergy and Spouses

Using a heuristic research method with negative case analysis means that the questions changed somewhat from person to person. As new issues unfolded, I pursued them in future interviews. However, the following are some of the basic questions that were asked in the interviews. Whether or not I asked some of these questions obviously was dependent on the person's previous answer or the particular circumstances (e.g married or single). Each person had filled out a questionnaire (Appendix II) prior to the interview.

1. Gave introductory information and built trust by:
    a. Telling some of my background and experience
    b. Describing aim, scope, method and assumptions of my research
    c. Assuring confidentiality.

2. Was there anything you learned or had highlighted in the process of filling out the qustionnaire?

3. The questionnaire responses were heavily weighted on the side that clergy and their spouses often have difficulty finding persons to talk to regarding personal issues. Not all felt that way, of course. Would you share what your experience has been. Why do you think that has been so for you?

4. One study indicates that if clergy do not have adequate support they tend to emotionally isolate themselves. Eighty-one percent of the clergy polled in that study experienced a sense of isolation in the ministry. Some people I talk with disagree. What's your experience been during the time you've been in the parish ministry? (If isolation) What do you see to be the causes of isolation?

5. One of my learnings from this questionnaire was confirmed by another study—namely that many clergy and spouses use their spouse as their primary support. Is this true for you? Or have you found your primary support somewhere else or more evenly spread among several sources? If your spouse is the key support and you are for her/him, what are the positive and negative effects on your marriage? Does being the major support for your spouse ever feel like a burden? One couple indicated that they were greatly relieved

when they each got into a counseling relationship, since it took the full load off of them.

6. Think of a key time in your life since you've been in the parish ministry when you especially needed personal support. How did you go about getting that support? (step by step) What got in the way of you getting the support you needed? (Check out attitudes, professional expectations, system, availability of resources.) Do you think that the size or location of your church was a factor in your finding or not finding support? Is it an issue that you could talk about with members of you parish? Why? Why not? Is it an issue you would take to your Conference minister? Why? Why not? Are there issues you can't take to either Conference Ministers or parishoners? Where do you go then?

7. I'm interested in learning what I can about how clergy support each other, both individually and in groups. What has been your experience? Have you ever belonged to a clergy support group? What was your experince in this setting? What helps or gets in the way of clergy supporting each other?

8. How do you feel about needing or asking for support? My questionnaire indicated that many find it difficult. Why do you think this is? One clergyperson put it this way. "We should be able to work this out for ourselves. We should be able to handle this if we have more faith." How do you react to that statement? Do you think that ministers and their spouses are any different than other people in their need for support? Is there anything in you that thinks they should be different because they are in a religious vocation?

9. More clergy checked spiritual dryness as an issue than any other on the questionnaire. One study showed that the longer someone is in the ministry, the more important it becomes to have resources for spiritual nourishment. How has this been for you? The same study indicated that many clergy feel least supported in this area. What are your key resources for spiritual nourishment? What do you think you need more of? Is there any one you share your spiritual journey with? Is this important?

10. For some clergy (spouses) there seem to be key points in their life and ministry where they needed extra support. . . .perhaps they corresponded to ages and stages like first parish, or mid-life, or transitions in marriage and family relationships. Can you think of key points during your ministry when you were in special need of

support? Were there resources available to you at these junctures? Whom? Where? Other resources besides people? e.g books, continuing education, retreats, conferences, denominationally supported events, marriage enrichment?

11. Stress and burnout seem to be issues for many people in our society these days. Is this an issue for you? What are the special factors for clergy regarding stress and burnout? How do you try to protect yourself from it? Do you feel like you have enough time for yourself and your family?

12. (For those persons who are single, ordained women, or homosexual) How does this affect you in finding the support you need?

13. What advice would you give to a clergyperson or clergy spouse just starting out in ministry regarding what they need to do to be sure they get the support they need for their lives and their ministry?

14. (Specifically for spouses) What is the best part of being a spouse of a clergyperson? What have been the hardest parts? How do you think that being married to a clergyperson has affected the ways you find support? In what ways do you feel supported by the denominational system? Does your support system include other clergy spouses? Do you wish it did?

The Alban Institute:
an invitation to membership

The Alban Institute, begun in 1979, believes that the congregation is essential to the task of equipping the people of God to minister in the church and the world. A multi-denominational membership organization, the Institute provides on-site training, educational programs, consulting, research, and publishing for hundreds of churches across the country.

The Alban Institute invites you to be a member of this partnership of laity, clergy, and executives—a partnership that brings together people who are raising important questions about congregational life and people who are trying new solutions, making new discoveries, finding a new way of getting clear about the task of ministry. The Institute exists to provide you with the kinds of information and resources you need to support your ministries.

Join us now and enjoy these benefits:

CONGREGATIONS, The Alban Journal, a highly respected journal published six times a year, to keep you up to date on current issues and trends.

Inside Information, Alban's quarterly newsletter, keeps you informed about research and other happenings around Alban. Available to members only.

Publications Discounts:

- [ ] 15% for Individual, Retired Clergy, and Seminarian Members
- [ ] 25% for Congregational Members
- [ ] 40% for Judicatory and Seminary Executive Members

Discounts on Training and Education Events

Write our Membership Department at the address below or call us at 1-800-486-1318 or 301-718-4407 for more information about how to join The Alban Institute's growing membership, particularly about Congregational Membership in which 12 designated persons receive all benefits of membership.

The Alban Institute, Inc.
Suite 433 North
4550 Montgomery Avenue
Bethesda, MD 20814-3341